SAINTS *of* *our* TIME

from EDITH STEIN *to* OSCAR ROMERO

JOHN MURRAY

First published in 2015 by Messenger Publications

ISBN 9781910248140

Designed by Messenger Publications Design Department
Typeset in Trajan and Baskerville
Printed by Naas Printing Ltd

Messenger Publications,
37 Lower Leeson Street, Dublin 2
www.messenger.ie

SAINTS

The universal call to holiness may have been particularly emphasised in the Second Vatican Council, but the call to sanctity has always been at the heart of the Church. We see the work of God's grace in the lives of so many holy children, women and men, right from the earliest years of the Church. It was not without good reason that St Paul called all believers 'saints'.

But saints come in all shapes and sizes. Some joker said that *'every saint has a bee in his halo!'* And that confident restlessness has come out in different ways. Many of them were fools for Christ's sake. Others acted heroically. Lots of them got to God by the scenic route, as the divine sculptor carved beauty from the hard rock of their lives. And we find many everyday saints who just did normal things with abnormal generosity.

Fr John Murray has a great eye to see the hands of the potter, forming and reforming the lives of all of these individuals, whether canonised or not. His stories of homely and heroic saints have delighted many for years.

As you read about these little masterpieces of God's grace:

May all that splendid company/ Whom Christ in glory came to meet/
Help us on our uneven road/ Made smoother by their passing feet.
(From the hymn in the Prayer of the Church for the Feast of All Saints)

+ Donal McKeown
Bishop of Derry

Contents

CHIARA LUCE BADANO

She had wanted to be an airhostess and see the world. She dreamed of marriage and having a family. She hoped to be a doctor and bring help and relief to children in Africa. And yet Chiara Luce Badano achieved none of the above but died before she was nineteen years of age and today is a Blessed of the Church.

In the traumatic years after the Second World War, Italy was trying to recover its economic and national strength and also its values. The war had been very divisive within Italian society. People were questioning within this traditionally Catholic country. Where had God been in the midst of the conflict? One young woman who tried to provide some answers was another Chiara, by the name of Lubich.

In the industrial heartland that was Turin, which had suffered a lot of bombing, Chiara launched a challenge to the rising new generation of young people who were looking to rebuild and move away from the entrenched positions of their parents. 'You must become a generation of saints,' she wrote. 'To build new cities and a new world, engineers, scientists and politicians are not enough; we need wise people, we need saints.' Out of the ruins of Turin arose the Focolare Movement and its secret: Jesus in the moment of his greatest suffering when he cried the abandonment of the Father. 'Without Him we cannot stand on our feet', the foundress wrote.

Chiara Badano had had some introduction through her parents to the nascent movement. She had participated in the Family Fest, an international event for families promoted by the Focolarini, as they were soon called. However, it was as a thirteen year old that she heard Chiara's clarion call to sanctity and it touched her heart deeply.

Prior to all this, however, Chiara was a normal little girl who was just the same as every other girl in the village – and yet different. Her parents had waited and prayed for eleven years before she arrived and when she came they loved her immensely but did not spoil her. Once when Chiara had stolen an apple from a neighbour's tree, her mother did not indulge her child's selfishness, but told her to go to the neighbour and apologise. The little girl was reluctant, but obeyed in the end. That evening, the woman, the tree owner, brought her a whole box of apples, saying that on that day Chiara had 'learnt something very important.'

At school she struggled, as anyone can. She sometimes had to repeat exams. Sometimes she was teased because of her beliefs; some even gave her the nickname 'sister', but nevertheless she had many friends and she socialised with them whenever she could. She also enjoyed the usual pastimes of music and dancing, as well as being a keen tennis player and swimmer.

By the age of sixteen, she had started to correspond regularly with the other Chiara, the founder of the movement. She even asked the older woman for a new name as this was going to be the start of a new life for her. Lubich replied by giving her the name 'Luce' which means 'light' in Italian. It was a sort of play on words for Chiara's own name means 'clear' in that same language. As Lubich would later write 'your luminous face shows your love for Jesus', which is why she gave her this new name.

Chiara Luce might well have gone on to take vows in the young movement like many others at that time – and since. Today Focolarini are all over the world in hundreds of small communities. But at the age of 17 something unexpected happened. While playing tennis she felt a sharp pain in her shoulder. She was admitted to hospital and the doctors' diagnosis was that she had cancer and that it was incurable. They recommended chemotherapy.

Chiara's mother relates a significant moment in the young girl's life and struggle to come to terms with what was happening. Maria Theresa said:

> I could see her at a distance. She was walking very slowly and her hands were in her pockets. Chiara entered the house; her face had a grim look. "Now, do not talk" she said to me and then threw herself on the bed. I wanted to say so many things – "you are young…you'll see …maybe.." But I could see there was a real struggle going on inside her.
>
> On the small shelf above her bed was a clock. After twenty-five minutes – I looked at the clock – she turned to me with her usual radiant smile and said – twice – "Mum, now you can speak." It took Chiara twenty-five minutes to say "yes" to God but she never went back on it.

There were difficult days ahead. She lost the power of her legs and once suffered a severe haemorrhage. Yet she survived a further year. 'Physically I suffer a lot,' she said,' but my soul sings. 'Often those who visited her came to cheer her up but left deeply affected by her serenity and peace. Some commented that Chiara's room was like a little touch of heaven. One doctor, a non-believer and a strong critic of the Church said 'something has changed inside me. There is coherence here and now I can understand Christianity.'

Shortly before she died on October 7 1990, she greeted personally everyone present. She said to them, 'I can no longer run but I would like to pass on to you the torch as one does in the Olympics. We have only one life and it is worth spending well.' Then she touched her mother's hair and said 'be happy because I am happy.' Chiara was declared 'Venerable' on July 3 2008 and 'Blessed' by the Church on September 25 2010. More than 20,000 young people were present in Rome for the event. In her few short years, Chiara had taught them how to live.

BOB BEDARD

I am writing these thoughts around the time of Pentecost. The story from Ephesians 19 comes up every year in one of the Mass readings just before the Sunday – 'Have you received the Holy Spirit?' Paul asks. The disciples' answer always intrigues me – and translations do vary – 'we haven't even heard there is a Holy Spirit' says one text – or 'we haven't heard one can receive the Holy Spirit' says another. Sometimes our parishes are a lot like that. Do our parishes need the Holy Spirit? Have we even heard one can receive the Holy Spirit? I leave the question for you, dear reader, to answer.

I never knew Bob Bedard personally but I did know people who knew him, priests who heard him and who were inspired by him. It is almost a year since his death and I wanted this month to remember him and the gifts and graces he brought to the Church, and in particular his openness to the work of the Holy Spirit.

I could identify with Bob. Like him I had taught for years in a school, though not quite as long as him. When finally the bishop 'released' him and gave him a new task – an inner city parish in Ottawa, Canada – I could recognise some of the challenges he faced. The skills he had honed in front of a blackboard – all chalk and talk – no digital technology or interactive whiteboards for him – seemed irrelevant in a rundown area which strong and traditional Catholics had long left in order to begin afresh in the leafy suburbs. Only the 'losers' and the poor seemed to stay behind.

There is always a danger when a new priest comes to a parish that he arrives with an agenda – 'his ideas' and 'his plan' to renew the parish. Perhaps Fr Bob was blessed to arrive with no such plan or programme. So he did nothing even though he was well known in the Charismatic circles of Canada at that time. He just celebrated Mass and the sacraments and waited on the Lord.

Yet as he prayed Bob felt he heard the Lord say something that was unusual. 'I don't want you to get into programmes. Give me permission to move freely here. Get as many people as possible to give me permission.' That is what Bob heard in his own spirit as he prayed and listened. 'Give me permission.'

Easier said than done. We like the idea of running a course or a programme in the parish or letting someone else do it. We are glad to try out something that perhaps a nearby colleague has seen work – Alpha, Cursillo, Life in the Spirit seminars etc. We don't want to be seen as lazy. The zealous parish priest wants to encourage all sorts of initiatives and types of spirituality from rosary groups to Padre Pio prayer, from Legion of Mary to Marriage Encounter. There is room for all. Fr Bob just waited. He felt he was a little like the Hebrews of old who waited on the Lord in the desert – when the fire moved they moved, and when it stopped they did too.

Fr Bob certainly had a lot of faith for he waited two years. Then God began to act – slowly but surely. People began to get converted at Mass. People commented on his sermons or how a text of scripture had touched them. Infrequent attenders began to come more regularly. Some who had been 'passive' Catholics began to experience something of the Holy Spirit in their lives. Some even began to cry in church, including some of the men. Bob was intrigued with this particular phenomenon. 'Why tears?' he asked, and in his prayer he felt God tell him that that was what was happening when people gave

Him permission. They were being brought to a deeper awareness of *who* He was and who they were before Him.

Soon the Masses became more vibrant as people began to praise God and not be embarrassed by singing out loud. There were some who were uncomfortable with this new 'liturgy', but most liked it and stayed. St Mary's was a parish that was beginning to attract people and to bring people back who had fallen away or who had lost a sense of direction. Attendances more than doubled.

There was another phenomenon that happened that also intrigued Bob – and that was the beginning of an interest in the priesthood. For many years he had taught in a Catholic high school and he had taught and counselled thousands of young men. No one had ever become a priest. Now young men were knocking on his door and asking for help and discernment. Bob took this particular feature as a sign that God was doing something really genuine in his parish. Soon the group of young priests and seminarians became known as the Companions of the Cross. They are still going strong to this day, with over 40 priests and six religious sisters.

I am privileged every so often to be asked to give the fifth evening in the 'Life in the Spirit' seminars. Participants have heard various talks, which outline the basic kerygma of the Gospel, and then on that fifth night they go forward to be prayed with for the 'baptism in the Spirit'. More and more I find myself telling people that they already have the Spirit – in Baptism and Confirmation – and now it is just a question of letting the Spirit take control. Just 'give God permission' – as Bob Bedard did – and then enjoy what the Spirit will do in you and in your parish.

JOSEPH BERNARDIN

I will never forget that moment. It was May 2009 and the Church's 'Year of Vocation' had come to an end. I gathered in a restaurant with a few sisters, priests and lay people who had worked hard during the year in order to promote vocations in the Church. It was a time of celebration and fraternity. We did not notice the man with a glass in his hand as he wandered over to our group and to me in particular; and after a couple of disarming pleasantries he let loose a string of crude and insulting comments. The sisters gasped, the waiters rushed to calm things down. I was speechless. It was the day after the Ryan report, on institutional abuse in the reformatory schools of Ireland, and feelings in the country were running high. I just happened to be in the wrong place at the wrong time.

My hurt was nothing; indeed it was good for my soul. The sins against the children over the decades *are* a blot on the Church's face and one that has affected the Church in the present age. Yet allow me to dwell this month on one man who was accused wrongly and was able to stay silent before his accuser.

Back in November 1993 a young man, a former seminarian, accused an American Cardinal of molesting him. The Cardinal in question, Joseph Bernardin, immediately denied the charges but rather than launch a counter attack he insisted that his case be submitted to the same process of investigation that he had established for others.

He refused to impugn the young man's character or do anything that might in any way discourage genuine victims of abuse from coming forward at that time.

To appreciate this moment in the recent history of the American Church we need to go back a little to see who Joseph Bernardin was and the important position he held in the Church at that time. He had been born in 1928 to an Italian immigrant couple. Initially he wanted to become a doctor, but soon recognised that his calling was to the priesthood. Ordination came in 1952 for the diocese of Charleston. His ministry was mainly in the diocese, as chancellor and vicar general. Within 14 years the young Joseph was ordained bishop, becoming the youngest in America at that time.

For two years Joseph served as the auxiliary bishop of Atlanta, but then in 1968 he became the first General secretary of the National Conference of American Bishops. He was instrumental in shaping the Church in the States and trying to implement the vision of the Second Vatican Council. It was a difficult time and Bernardin found himself as a mediator between the diverging parties of the post-Conciliar Church.

Further promotions followed – archbishop of Cincinnati in 1972 and then Archbishop of Chicago in 1982. With this came the red hat of a Cardinal. He also served on a number of Vatican commissions as he worked to improve relations between Catholics and Jews and also between Catholics and other Christians.

One of his key initiatives was in drafting 'The Challenge of Peace', the Bishops' pastoral letter on nuclear war. It was the most significant statement ever issued by the hierarchy on public policy and it raised much controversy for its strong condemnation of nuclear war and its critical treatment of American military policies. According to Bernardin, the Church's commitment to the sacredness of life was a 'seamless garment' that integrated opposition to abortion with opposition to capital punishment and euthanasia, concern for peace and social justice and a commitment to the poor and the most helpless in society.

While he was in Chicago the first beginnings of the clerical abuse scandals were raising their head. Bernardin implemented a policy in the diocese, which served as a model for other dioceses across the nation. Too often in the past, people had been afraid to come forward with allegations. They just thought that no one would believe them. Bernardin wanted to assure victims that this would no longer be the case. When in November 1993 someone accused him, he had to undergo the same process he had established for others in the diocese.

The charges were widely publicised; the media had a field day. Some privately sneered at how another hypocrite had been unmasked. Yet three months later the story took a different turn when the accuser withdrew the charges, acknowledging that his 'memories were unreliable'. He apologised to Bernardin. The Cardinal met privately with the young man, who by this time was dying of AIDS and he forgave him. Bernardin's courage was not just an example for the victims but also for priests throughout the world.

There was to be another sequel: cancer had developed in Bernardin's pancreas. In 1995 he underwent surgery and afterwards began a new ministry – to those who were suffering from cancer. Hundreds were touched in this final time and Bernardin even wrote a book about the end of life called '***The Gift of Peace***'.

In September 1996 he made a final pilgrimage to Rome – to see Pope John Paul II – and also to visit Assisi. A few weeks later he passed away.

A final postscript: about a year after that first event mentioned at the beginning of this piece, I was walking across a large car park on a late November evening. It was dark but there was enough streetlight to be able to see. Suddenly a loud voice shouted out 'Hey, are you a priest?' My heart stopped – 'not again' I thought. I fidgeted with my scarf to see if I could cover my collar. Tentatively I approached the man and waited for his next sentence. 'Yes, I am.' I said. 'Good,' he replied. 'I want to talk to a priest.'

The rest of our conversation is between him and God.

ANDRE BESSETTE

Anyone familiar with the story of Solanus Casey, the porter in the Detroit (Michigan) monastery, will recognise traits in the story also of Andre Bessette of Montreal in Canada. They were both doorkeepers, assigned a simple task which it was felt would be fitting to their perceived limited abilities. Yet each in their own way had a powerful ministry, which reached beyond the confines of their monastic homes and touched the lives of countless men and women.

Alfred (later Andre in religious life) was born in Montreal in Canada in 1845. He was the eighth of twelve children. Sadly his parents died when he was only twelve years of age – his father in a work accident and his mother of tuberculosis, a common illness at that time not just in Canada, but also here in Ireland. So Alfred was adopted and he had to learn quickly how to earn his keep. His early years of work included being a farmhand and he also turned to shoemaking, baking and even being a blacksmith. During the boom times, which followed the end of the American Civil War, he worked in the United States in a factory.

However, at the age of twenty-five, Andre applied to enter the Congregation of the Holy Cross as a working brother. The community almost dismissed him at the end of the novitiate because he was rather sickly but the Archbishop of the city intervened and asked them to keep him. He is reported as saying 'I am sending you a saint'. Religious communities know that they are called to holiness but they can sometimes be suspicious when they see it in action. It is easier to recognise a saint when he or she is dead. Living saints can be awkward. Andre's superiors decided to give this frail and rather uneducated young man the simplest of tasks. 'They showed me the door,' quoted Andre, 'and I stayed there for forty years.'

Andre combined this basic task at the monastery with other roles – sacristan, laundry worker and messenger boy. Nothing was too menial for him and he was always glad to serve. However, it was at the door that his ministry blossomed. In his little room near the door, he spent many hours on his knees. Soon he began to hear of people in need especially those who were sick. He would visit, taking with him some oil that he took from the sanctuary lamp in the monastery chapel, and he would rub the oil lightly on the wound or sore area where appropriate. He combined this ministry with a great devotion to St Joseph and kept a small statue of the saint on his windowsill. 'Some day Joseph is going to be honoured in a very special way on Mount Royal', he would say when asked about his devotion.

When an epidemic broke out at a nearby college, Andre volunteered to help, and not one person died. The trickle of sick people at the beginning became a flood. Some of his better-educated colleagues were uneasy with the constant crowd of people hanging around the schoolyard. His superiors were uneasy too and the diocesan authorities suspicious. Even some of the local doctors called him a 'quack' – 'I do not cure,' he said. 'Joseph cures.' And so the healings and the cures continued – so much so that towards the end of his life he needed four secretaries to help him deal with the 80,000 letters he was receiving from people all over the North American continent.

Traditionally the congregation had a devotion to St Joseph; so Andre's own devotion was not unique. However he went further in promoting Joseph as an aid for many people. For many years the Holy

Cross authorities had tried in vain to buy land on Mount Royal (Montreal). Andre and some others climbed the hill and planted medals of St Joseph at various places and soon after the owners gave in and sold the property. In time this became a practice for people who wanted to buy or sell a home. For his part, Andre raised money to build an oratory there and it was there that he was able to receive visitors and listen to their problems and pray with them for healing. The chapel is still in use today.

Today the spirit of Andre continues not just in Montreal but also wherever the congregation exists the people come – those who are struggling with drugs, people who have suffered sexual abuse, those just out of prison. Everyday the brothers are confronted with what seem like insurmountable problems but then they remember the faith of Andre. Because he could not read, Andre memorised the scriptures, particularly the Beatitudes, and always tried to apply the lessons of the faith shown in the Gospels to the persons who stood before him seeking help.

Doing the ordinary things in an extraordinary way. That was the key to Andre's witness. The spiritual writers of the 18th century like Jean Pierre de Caussade and others would have encouraged his living 'in the present moment' for it is there that we clarify God most. God is present in that man or woman at the door who needs our ear and our time. The people of Montreal knew this and when Andre died on January 6 1937, more than a million pilgrims passed his coffin. His feast day is celebrated each January on his anniversary.

DIETRICH BONHOEFFER

The whole camp had to watch as two men died by hanging. But the third was a boy, just into his teens, and his body weight meant that death did not come instantaneously – mercifully. He hung for what seemed like ages, gasping for breath. 'Where is God in all this?' Elie heard an angry voice in a row behind him.

The story is taken from Elie Wiesel's short story 'Night', which tells something of his time – and survival – in the notorious death camp of Auschwitz. Some time before, in another land, a young man asked himself, 'What am I doing here?' I'm sure that is a question many of us have asked ourselves at some time or other.

This young man was perhaps no different from Cyprian, Bishop of Carthage, at the height of the Decian persecution in 250, encouraged to flee the Emperor's troops in order to ensure survival. He was no different from Peter on the way out of Rome, persuaded to flee by his fellow Christians. 'It would not be good if you, the leader, were caught', they argued. The fire of Rome and the mad anger of the Emperor Nero seemed logical to Peter until he met Jesus, tradition tells us, on the road to Rome. 'Quo Vadis?' ('where are you going?') Peter asked. The answer Jesus gave made Peter turn on his heel and return to the city eventually to be crucified.

Dietrich Bonhoeffer – the young man – spent the month of June 1939 in the city of New York in a state of soul-searching. 'I do not know why I am here' he wrote. Some American friends eager to protect the young Lutheran theologian from the clutches of the Gestapo had arranged for him to serve as a visiting professor at one of the leading theology seminaries in the country. Bonhoeffer had been an avowed enemy of the Nazis, and certainly the move to America had saved his life. But after only a few weeks, he surprised his friends by planning to return. 'I will have no right to participate in the reconstruction of Christian life in Germany after the war if I do not share the tribulations of this time with my people,' he told them.

Ironically when Dietrich returned he did not throw himself into any obvious opposition but instead joined the German Military Intelligence (Abwehr). However, his brother-in-law, Hans Dohnanyi, was a leading member of this organisation and was aware of Dietrich's thoughts. He inducted him into the clandestine conspiracy to overthrow Hitler.

In 1943, both men were arrested with others but even then the extent of the plan – which included the assassination of Hitler – was unknown. While investigations were being made, Bonhoeffer was remanded to a military prison where he remained for 18 months. It was not a concentration camp and so the conditions were not spartan and he was able to receive books and send out uncensored letters. However, the end was coming soon.

In July 1944, a complete assassination plot ended in failure. It featured in recent years in the film *Valkyrie* (2008) starring Tom Cruise. When the Gestapo realised the extent of the plot, the fate of the conspirators was sealed. Bonhoeffer was sent to Buchenwald camp and then to Flossenburg, where on the evening of April 9 he conducted a final prayer service for his fellow prisoners. A last note to a fellow prisoner read 'this is the end, for me the beginning of life.' The next day he was hanged along with five others.

Bonhoeffer did not leave a massive corpus of work. Indeed his *Let-*

ters and Papers from Prison remains his biggest legacy. However, his impact has been felt at different levels. In letters smuggled out to his friend, Eberhard Bethge, he outlined the need for a new 'religionless Christianity', a way of talking about God in a secular age. For him, traditional religious language had tended to posit a stop-gap God occupying a sort of religious realm on the edge of daily life. He wrote:

> Religious people speak of God when human knowledge has come to an end, the "*Deus ex machina*". It always seems to me that we are trying anxiously in this way to reserve some space for God. I should like to speak of God not on the boundaries but at the centre, not in weaknesses but in strength and therefore not in death and guilt but in man's life and goodness. God is beyond in the midst of our life. The Church stands not at the boundaries where human powers give out, but in the midst of the village.

Some have attributed – partially – to Bonhoeffer the later rise of the 'God is Dead' movement, which grew out of the ashes of a beaten and war weary Europe. How could a good God allow such evil, such massive suffering? Coupled with some of the scripture scholarship of the age there were those who suggested that to be a Christian was to simply be a follower of Jesus of Nazareth, who was long since dead but whose values and witness to truth one could adhere to. For them, a supernatural God was truly dead.

And yet this was not being true to Bonhoeffer. He really did believe that God was present totally in the midst of people's sufferings and pains, even if He did not seem to remove them, or at times seemed deaf to their pain.

And so back to my initial story – a concentration camp, a commandant who wanted to make an example, and three unfortunate victims who paid with their lives. 'Where is God in all this?' the man behind asked. Then suddenly Wiesel realised – that there was God, dangling on the end of that rope.

TITUS BRANDSMA

If you had met Titus Brandsma in his first sixty years, you would not necessarily have been left feeling that you had been in the presence of a saint. Yes, he was a good priest and diligent teacher, but the stuff of sainthood? Indeed a Dutch journalist who wrote a book about Titus in 2008 spoke of his vanity and short temper, while acknowledging also that he was a man of true charity and great personal courage. God's saints are not always perfect nor would they claim to be.

Anno Sjoerd (Titus became his name in religion later, although it was also his father's name) was born in 1881. His background was rural and he was indeed a willing worker but somehow his physique was not quite up to the demands of a diary farm. Despite this, Anno never shirked his share of the daily work. From an early age he had entertained the idea of a religious vocation and with his parents' permission entered the Franciscan minor seminary at the early age of eleven – such was the custom in the Church then.

However, over the next six years, he found the rigours of the Franciscan life too hard and was advised to leave. He was accepted by the Carmelite Fathers and after the required training and formation was ordained as a priest in his native Holland in 1905. There are horses for courses, it is often said, and this was so true in the case of Titus. From the beginning of his time with the Carmelites his gifts came to the fore. He showed an extraordinary talent for journalism and writing, and indeed translated the works of St Teresa of Avila from Spanish into Dutch. His interest in mysticism ultimately led him to travel to France, Germany, Italy, Spain and the United States and in 1935 was named by the bishops of Holland as national spiritual adviser to Catholic journalists.

For many years, Fr Titus taught philosophy and theology at the Catholic university of Nijmegen, which the Dutch bishops had established in 1923. He also formed schools for boys and helped to reform the Carmelite seminary curriculum. And in addition he edited a journal on spirituality. Almost as a personal hobby, he established a library of mediaeval spiritual manuscripts, which included three hundred editions of the great classic *The Imitation of Christ*. All in all it was the sort of life and busyness that many priest-teachers have experienced the world over through the ages.

However, it was at the age of sixty that Titus made his most significant contribution. When the Nazis invaded Holland and very quickly subdued it, the Catholic bishops commissioned him to unite the Catholic press against these invaders. He drafted a letter urging all editors to refuse to publish any Nazi material or propaganda. No Catholic publication, he wrote, could publish Nazi propaganda and still call itself Catholic. He personally delivered the letter to fourteen of the most important Catholic papers in the country. He had already come to the attention of the Nazis in 1935 when he had written against anti-Jewish laws, which had been promulgated in the country. This further act consolidated their suspicion of him.

He was promptly arrested and placed in a jail at Scheveningen. The date was January 19 1942. One official told him that he admired his courage but regarded him as 'a very dangerous person'. For several weeks he was shuttled from jail to jail and eventually to the notorious Dachau concentration camp which was often the last residence for many priests and regime dissidents. There he was overworked and underfed. Often he was beaten daily. The kidney infections from which he suffered often during the 1930s surfaced more frequently and Titus often found himself in the camp infirmary. Even then Titus tried to minister to the other prisoners, much in the same way that Maximilian Kolbe did in Auschwitz almost at the same time. When he could no longer work he was used for medical experiments and when these too were exhausted he was administered a lethal drug of acid on July 26 1942, which killed him within a few minutes. His executioner was a nurse who had been raised Catholic and who had left the Church. Despite the cruelty of this act Titus managed somehow to give the nurse a rosary. One would like to think that it had some lasting and eternal effect in the life of the executioner.

Titus – ever the writer – did not waste his time in Dachau but tried to write in so far as his circumstances allowed. Much of those camp writings have been lost to posterity but enough survived to give the lasting impression of a man who was able to live a life of joy in the midst of incredible evil and who did not seek martyrdom but bowed with humility to it when it sought him. 'We are here,' he wrote, 'in a dark tunnel. We must pass through it. Somewhere at the end shines the eternal light.' With a love that only Christ could give he was able to forgive his enemies.

Pope John Paul beatified Titus on November 3 1985 – the first victim of the Nazis to be officially declared a martyr – and his feast day is celebrated on July 27. In 2005 the citizens of Nijmegen in Holland chose him as the greatest citizen who had lived there.

PRAYER: God our Father, source of life and freedom, through your Holy Spirit you gave the Carmelite Titus Brandsma the courage to affirm human dignity even in the midst of suffering and degrading persecution. Grant us that same Spirit so that refusing all compromise with error we may always and everywhere give coherent witness to your abiding presence among us.

We ask this through Christ our Lord. Amen.

CARLO CARRETTO

Lent has a long-standing tradition in our Church. Many of us enter into it full of good intentions and with a decision made as to how we will live it. If we are honest however, many of us arrive at Easter not really having begun. I know that happens to me. The Church calls us to 'go into the desert' with Jesus – to fast for forty days – in whatever form that takes. Some will go off the 'black stuff' while others will skip chocolate or sweets. When I was growing up I admired the men in my village, who drank all year but every Lent abstained completely. I know of one priest who takes the plug out of the back of the TV on Ash Wednesday and does not return it until Easter Sunday. Could you do that? Everyone has their own way of doing Lent.

The man I wish to remember with this article literally went into the desert in his search for God and bequeathed to the Church of his time – and later – much needed wisdom. Carlo Carretto began life on April 2 1910 in Northern Italy and after graduating as a teacher he became involved in the work of Catholic Action in his native land. For twenty years his life was a blur of talks and conferences, meetings and travel up and down the length and breadth of his country and even abroad. He was a gifted leader and gave valuable direction to the movement at a time when the allegiance of young people was being swayed by the Fascism of Mussolini and others.

Then – suddenly – he left it all and joined the Little Brothers of Charles de Foucauld. In explaining his decision he said he felt a call from God: 'leave everything and come with me into the desert. It is not your acts and deeds that I want; I want your prayer, your love.' And so in December 1954, at the age of 44 Carlo arrived in El Abiodh, an oasis in the middle of Algeria, to begin a novitiate with the Little Brothers. He remained there for ten years – a period of prayer and reflection and indeed much writing.

In his *Letters from the Desert* Carlo sought to explain the spirituality of Charles de Foucauld, who too had tried to emulate Jesus during his anonymous years in Nazareth. For Carretto the desert was a place of encounter with God and a testing of faith. Ultimately he believed that the encounter with God must lead us back to the midst of our fellow human beings. So, in 1964 he found himself back in a new experimental community in Spello, Italy. In the next two decades Carlo's reputation spread through his books and retreats. He even gained a certain degree of notoriety, and the displeasure of some Church authorities because of his criticism of clericalism and affluence in the Church. But always there was loyalty: 'No, I shall not leave this Church, founded on so frail a rock, because I should be founding another one on an even frailer rock: myself.' Indeed his own spirit was so close to that of Francis of Assisi, who loved the Church and so much wanted to see it renewed. Carlo even died on the feast of Francis – October 4 1988.

During his reign, Pope Benedict wrote a letter to the Church in Ireland. It related of course to the terrible abuse by clerics of children. In it he invited the Catholics of Ireland to devote their Friday penances for one year until Easter 2011: 'I ask you to offer up your fasting, your prayer, your reading of scripture and your works of mercy in order to obtain the grace of healing and renewal for the Church in Ireland.' Have we been faithful to this request from our Holy Father?

I know my own response has not been as wholehearted as it should have been, and I scarcely hear anybody else talking about it or doing anything in obedience to this holy word. I know too that many rejected and even ridiculed Benedict's request from the start. Yet it is not too late to start – and maybe the next Lent will be the time.

Carretto too loved the Church, but also knew well its faults. One of his most famous writings is his 'Love Letter to the Church.' Here is a paraphrased excerpt:

> How much I must criticise you, my Church and yet how much I love you! You have made me suffer more than anyone and yet I owe you more than I owe anyone. I should like to see you destroyed and yet I need your presence. You have given me much scandal and yet you alone have made me understand holiness. Never in the world have I seen anything more compromised, more false, yet never have I touched anything more pure, more generous, or more beautiful. Countless times I have felt like slamming the door of my soul in your face – and yet every night I have prayed that I might die in your arms! No, I cannot be free of you, for I am one with you, even if not completely you. Then too – where should I go? To build another Church? But I cannot build another Church without the same defects, for they are my defects. And again, if I were to build another Church, it would be my Church, not Christ's Church.

So I invite you, dear reader, to join me in whatever way you can by going into the desert for your next Lent. Fast as you can, try to pray and read the scriptures and above all seek the face of the Lord. And pray for the renewal of His Church that we all so love.

WALTER CISZEK

The article on bygone days featured a photo. The archivist author gently asked anyone if they knew the people in the photo so that they could be named. My father's cousin, a priest of over 60 years and a former student of the Irish College in Rome identified them. Initially I had recognised him but who were the others? They were Jesuits, he said. They had come to the Irish College one fine day in the late 1930s to celebrate Mass and then have lunch. Most of them were volunteering for the Russian mission, knowing that if they were caught they might never be heard of again. One of them was Walter Ciszek.

In 1947, the Jesuits in New York had also gathered to remember – and offer Mass for – Walter Ciszek, one of their priests who had gone missing in the Soviet Union and was presumed dead. In 1938 he had volunteered for such a mission and through working with Polish refugees he had somehow slipped into Russia and worked there for two years in a lumber yard, but carrying out as best he could the ministry of a priest. Then in 1941 he was arrested by the secret police and to all intents and purposes vanished. Yet he remained very much alive within the closed system of the Soviet Gulag.

The story of Walter Ciszek begins in 1904 in the mining town of Shenandoah in Pennsylvania. He was the son of Polish immigrants, Martin and Caroline who had come to the States in the 1890s. There was always something of a rebel in Walter – in his teens he had been a member of a gang. To everyone's surprise, he joined the Jesuits in 1928 and then quickly volunteered for the Soviet mission after Pope Pius XI had appealed to priests from around the world to go to Russia as missionaries. In 1934 he was sent to Rome for studies at the Russicum (Pontifical Russian College) and it was probably from there, one day many years ago, that my father's cousin met him with the others for prayer and lunch.

Ciszek spent five years in the notorious Lubianka prison in Moscow. He was known as a priest, but the police were determined to expose him as a spy. In his books (*He Leadeth Me* and *With God in Russia*) he outlined his regime, for apart from his interrogations he met no other human contact for all those years. Digging deep into the wells of his Jesuit training he mapped out his day, beginning with morning prayer followed by Mass (all enacted from memory); the Angelus which he knew from one of the local bells of the city; then the rosary and reflection on scripture. 'Lubianka was in many ways a school of prayer for me,' he later said.

Perhaps naively at the beginning, Walter thought he would be able to satisfy the police and so gain his freedom. Eventually he became resigned to the fact that there was nothing he could do to win his freedom. Exhausted and trusting totally in Providence, he signed a confession and was sentenced to fifteen years in Siberia. Incredibly, Walter realised that as long as he tried to struggle and resist his destiny, he felt tired and miserable – but to the extent that he abandoned himself to God, convinced that in every situation, he was where God wanted him to be. He felt a sense of peace and freedom.

Siberia was brutal – the piercing cold, the backbreaking work in the mines or ore processing plant, the roughness of some of the other prisoners. However, once they realised he was a priest, he became an unofficial chaplain to the camp. Even bread and wine were smuggled in for him to say Mass. 'For I was Christ in this prison camp' he wrote.

Even unbelievers sought him out and Walter found that each encounter with a prisoner was an opportunity to do the work of God.

Aside from the difficulties mentioned above, there was also a constant insecurity. Once after a prison revolt he was taken outside with some other prisoners to be shot. He tried to remember his act of Contrition as the soldiers raised their weapons – and then to his utter relief, the execution was halted. It was a devastating moment, but one which taught him to trust even more in the Lord: 'I realised that true freedom meant nothing else than letting God operate within my soul without interference.'

When the fifteen years were complete Walter was released – the year was 1955 – but it was a relative freedom. As a convicted felon, he had to stay in towns in Siberia, constantly under surveillance from the secret police. He worked in various kinds of menial labour, but again once his identity was known his services as a priest were on demand. And when he became too popular with this, the KGB moved him on to another town.

Eventually even this period came to an end and he was allowed a letter home to his astonished friends and family who thought he was long dead. In 1963 he was summoned without warning to Moscow and put on a plane and sent home – in exchange for a couple of Soviet spies. He arrived in New York on October 12, after 23 years in the Soviet Union. Ciszek lived on for another 20 years, teaching and providing spiritual direction to those who wanted. He remained extraordinarily free of bitterness toward the land of his captivity. He believed that the spiritual lessons he had learned during his ordeal were applicable to all people, whatever their circumstances. To those who asked what was the secret of his survival, he simply replied 'God's Providence', and if pressed further he would add the words of St Paul: 'if God is for us who can be against us?'

Father Walter Ciszek died on December 8 1984 at the age of eighty.

The Church has recognised his holiness and he is now officially 'a servant of God', the first rung on the ladder to canonisation and sainthood. It is fitting to end with one of his quotations, which was the key to his survival – 'the power of prayer reaches beyond all efforts of man seeking to find meaning in life. This power is available to all; it can transform man's weaknesses, limitations and his sufferings.'

CORNELIA CONNOLLY

You probably know the story about St Teresa! Once when crossing a stream on horseback, Teresa was tossed over the horse's head and landed in the water. 'If this is how you treat your friends, Lord, 'she said 'it is no wonder you have so few!'

Being recognised as a saint certainly does not mean that the person is spared any suffering or tribulation. This is certainly true of the person I wish to consider this month. However, the sufferings of Cornelia Connolly were perhaps very different from the normal ones of bodily pain and suffering. Her cross was to be of a more spiritual nature – through her marriage and, later, in her appearance.

Cornelia Peacock was born in 1809, to a wealthy Philadelphia family, which allowed her all the fruits of education and comfort that her status allowed. In 1831 she married an Episcopalian priest named Pierce Connolly. In time, Pierce studied and thought his way into the Catholic Church and Cornelia went with him. Cornelia was carried along by the strength of will of her husband, but a fledgling spirituality and call to personal holiness was growing. No doubt, she hoped to develop this through fidelity to her husband and children.

In those early years, the couple earned their living by teaching in the local Catholic schools. Three children had come quickly, while sadly a fourth – a little girl – died a few weeks after birth. Then worse was to come when their two year old, John, was pushed by a dog into a vat of boiling sugar cane juice. He died almost two days later. All the while that Cornelia held his scalded body, she was able to identify with the sorrowing Mary, who held Jesus in her arms beneath the cross. When John died on February 2, the feast of the Presentation, Cornelia wrote in her diary 'he was taken into the temple of the Lord.'

Then the story of Cornelia took a completely surprising direction. Pierce, having found his way into the Catholic Church, now wanted to become a priest. 'Is it necessary for Pierce to make this sacrifice and sacrifice me?' she asked of her own spiritual advisor. 'I love my husband; I love my darling children; why must I give them up?' She remained faithful – pregnant with her fifth child – while Pierce went off to Rome to study.

Eventually Pierce summoned his family to join him. He had been given permission to become a priest by Pope Gregory XVI, provided he remained celibate. So while Pierce pursued his studies, Cornelia lived in a convent close to the Spanish steps. He visited her once a week but to all intents and purposes she was quite alone. She wrote… 'incapable of listening or understanding or thinking… I forced my will to rejoice in the greatness of God.'

Life took on a new direction. Pierce was ordained in 1845 and Cornelia felt she should duly return to the United States. However some bishops suggested she go to England – a country that was emerging slowly from centuries of persecution and was experiencing a certain amount of renewal and expansion. Someone suggested her calling was to establish a new religious congregation for the education of girls. She accepted this new challenge, provided she could keep her own family with her. Soon she arrived in the city of Derby and took over a newly built convent school.

In 1847 Cornelia took religious vows herself, and Bishop Wiseman – later Cardinal – installed her as superior of her new congregation, the Society of the Holy Child Jesus. The name reflected her own spirituality and faith in the incarnation, specifically to the 'humbled God who had revealed himself in the form of a helpless child.' She would tell her sisters 'as you step through the muddy streets, love God with your feet; and when your hands toil, love Him with your hands; and you teach little children, love Him in his little ones.'

Yet now there was to be another twist to Cornelia's life. Pierce had become disenchanted with the priesthood and had become quite anti-Catholic in his writings. He even started to appear at her convent. He wanted her to resume their marital life and he even tried to interfere in the life of the congregation. Cornelia had followed him in earlier years and was happy in her role as his spouse, but now she was strong and confident in her role as a religious. She would no longer accept his word as the word of God. Pierce brought a suit against her in a high Anglican ecclesiastical court. He painted a picture of his wife as being 'a captive to the agents of Rome.' Despite this the court ruled in her favour. Enraged, Pierce kidnapped the children and took them out of the country. Cornelia would never see them again. For a mother it was the sorest blow of all.

She remained on as the superior of her congregation for over thirty more years. During this time she was able to see its growth in England and beyond to America and also to France. Today it is also in Africa. The congregation did much to promote the education of women, especially the poor. This was a source of great satisfaction to her, for she knew the benefits the education she had received as a result of her own family's wealth.

The final strand of suffering came in her latter years, as she experienced a bad case of eczema, which gave her the appearance of a leper. It was as though she had been scalded from head to foot. On the day before she died, on April 18 1879, in St Leonards-on-Sea in Sussex, she turned to the sister who was nursing her and said 'in this flesh I shall see my God!' In 1992 The Church declared Cornelia as Venerable.

PAUL COUTURIER

Fr Paul Couturier, an obscure schoolteacher from the city of Lyon in France, was one of the great pioneers of the ecumenical movement. Although he died in 1953 he could be called a precursor of the Second Vatican Council. His vision and understanding of the Christian unity were echoed in the Council documents on ecumenism but also later in the actions and teachings of the late Pope John Paul II.

Couturier taught a spiritual ecumenism, recognising that divisions between Churches and Christians were a spiritual problem requiring a spiritual solution. He taught the need for prayer and repentance. Although there was already in existence a 'Week of Prayer for Christian Unity', his work gave fresh impetus to this initiative.

He was born in 1881 in Lyon, and was ordained in the Society of St Irenaeus in 1906, a company of mission and teaching priests. A graduate in physical sciences, he became a teacher at the Society's school where he remained until 1946.

As a result of an Ignatian retreat in his early twenties, he was encouraged to take up some relief work among Lyon's many Russian refugees, which in turn, introduced him to Orthodoxy and a hitherto unknown world of spirituality and Church life.

Metropolitan Platon Gorodetsky (1803–1891) of Kiev had a saying, that 'the walls of separation do not rise as far as heaven', which became a principle of Couturier's ecumenical outlook. Strongly influenced also by the teaching of Dom Lambert Beauduin, he placed the prayerful celebration of the Church's liturgy at the heart of his spiritual life.

Paul believed that all Christians could unite in regular prayer and devotion, each according to their own tradition and insight, for the sanctification of the world and the unity of Christ's people. So was born the idea of 'the Invisible Monastery', a spiritual community, beyond the earth's 'walls of separation', where God's vision of his Church's unity could be realised.

Couturier was deeply struck that Jesus' prayer on the night before he died was not simply for his disciples' unity, but that they might be one as the Father and the Son are one, so that the world might believe. He realised that the unity of Christians was therefore a reality in heaven and that overcoming worldly divisions through penitence and charity would be to offer a renewed faith to the whole world. Merely human efforts would not prevail.

The power of prayer, and its potential for overcoming the wounds of centuries, lay at the heart of all Christian believers, and so he came to see that, as people grow in sanctity in their different traditions, they grow closer to Christ. If Christians could be aware of each other's spirituality and traditions, they could grow closer to each other.

In January 1933, during the Church Unity Octave, Couturier held three days of study and prayer. The Octave had been founded in 1906 by the Reverend Spencer Jones and Fr Paul Watson of the Friars of the Atonement (when still Anglicans) to pray for the reunion of Christians with the See of Rome. After the Friars became Roman Catholic, the observance was extended to the whole Church in 1916.

But Couturier wanted to build on the Octave something which could embrace in prayer those who were unlikely ever to become Roman Catholics but who nevertheless desired the end to separation and the achievement of visible unity.

In 1934, Couturier's new form was extended to a whole week, and the modern Week of Prayer for Christian Unity was born. The annual celebrations in Lyon, with their important speakers and high level ecumenical participation, become famous, attracting attention throughout Europe.

In 1936, the Abbe Couturier organised at Erlenbach in Switzerland the first interconfessional spiritual meeting, mainly of Catholic clergy and Reformed pastors, which was to meet in fellowship for many years and directly contributed to the foundations of the World Council. Two visits to England in 1937 and 1938 completed his initiation into ecumenism with the discovery of Anglicanism.

During the Second World War, largely on account of his extensive international contacts, Couturier was imprisoned by the Gestapo. This broke his health, but he identified his suffering as a cross, which he was being called to take up in the service of the unity of Christians. He continued to pray the liturgy of the Church, to make arrangements for the Week of Prayer and to sustain friendships around the world.

He lived to rejoice in the foundation of the World Council of Churches in the aftermath of the Second World War. Although his own Church did not join the new body at that time, his hope that Rome could lead an appeal for convergence was heard by Pope Pius and doubtless informed the forthcoming Council. He died in Lyon on March 24 1953.

At his funeral, the Archbishop of Lyon, Cardinal Gerlier, hailed him as the 'Apostle of Christian Unity'. He said:

There is no sterner commandment in the Gospel of our Lord Jesus Christ, whose prayer it was that they may all be one. It is the great scandal of the world that Christians are divided. All those who love Jesus Christ, those also who for love of Jesus Christ love their brethren, are homesick for the unity of Christians. It was to this task of unity that dear Pere Couturier dedicated his life, with a devotion and charity that were truly wonderful.

DOROTHY DAY

Having an abortion may not be part of the profile of most saints but, as we know, many of the greatest saints had unwholesome starts to their lives before they discovered the call of the Lord. Dorothy Day is not yet a canonised saint – although her cause has been introduced in Rome – but she is typically a 'saint' for the modern age.

Dorothy Day was born in 1897. One of her earliest memories was of the San Francisco earthquake in 1906, which devastated so much of the city. Her family lived in a suburb called Oakland, and so were spared much of the damage, but many refugees spilled out of the city, and Dorothy had an abiding memory of the kindness of the Oakland residents as they ministered to the needy.

A bright girl, she sailed through high school, and won a scholarship to the University of Illinois. She paid her way by washing dishes, and always thought herself lucky compared to the girls who worked in shops and factories with no prospect of advancement. After graduation, she began work as a newspaper reporter.

During the latter years of the First World War, Dorothy's principles would not allow her to don uniform, as so many of her contemporaries were doing. She thought, however, that she could be of some value by becoming a nurse.

It was then that she fell in love with one of her patients, a man called Lionel Moise. The relationship ended in sordid tragedy, however, when Dorothy became pregnant in May 1919. Lionel arranged for her to have an abortion and, while she was in the clinic, he left the apartment, never to be seen again.

Later, she began a relationship with another man, by whom she became pregnant in 1925. Like his predecessor, he was not ready for this and, as an atheist, was less than pleased when Dorothy in gratitude turned to God.

In March the following year, a little girl, Tamar Teresa, was born. Dorothy was determined to have her baptised, and to do so in the Catholic Church, which by this stage she felt was the Church of the poor. She hoped to receive the sacrament herself, but hesitated when she was told that she would have to live as a single parent.

God was moving in her life, however, as she wrote in her book, *The Long Loneliness*. 'Sooner or later one is given a chance to prove his love,' she wrote. 'No human creature could receive or contain so vast a flood of love as I felt after the birth of my child. With this came the need to worship.' The obstacle to Dorothy's baptism was removed when she and Tamar's father broke up.

Dorothy's life took on a new direction when a somewhat eccentric Frenchman, Peter Maurin, entered the scene. Once he had got Dorothy's attention, Peter began to share his view of the world with her, a view that fitted in very well with what she herself wanted. It was out of their shared enthusiasm that the 'houses of hospitality' began to appear, offering food and accommodation to those who needed it.

Dorothy's long-time love for the printed word also led to the formation of a newspaper, which Peter saw as an ideal tool for disseminating their ideas. And so *The Catholic Worker* was born on May Day, 1933.

By 1935, the newspaper had a run of 110,000 copies. Most found their way into parishes and schools, but Dorothy – ever the journalist – loved the idea of competing with other papers by selling it on the streets. By the following year, the paper was still growing and so were the houses – now thirty in number – in all parts of America, and one in England.

Her message was simple, and sometimes it shocked the stuffier women's clubs. Dorothy met the dispossessed farmers of the Mid-West, as well as the casual labourers of the fruit groves in California, and she was able to describe their sufferings in the columns of her paper. She brought home to the laity, as well as to the bishops of the Church, the Jesus of the gospels and his compassion for the poor.

The hungry thirties made many demands on the movement. Sometimes as many as a thousand people might be queuing for a meal. Donations kept flowing, but the organisation was always in debt and, when the coffers were empty, a delegation would go around to the local church and 'picket' St Joseph's statue. Miracles happened frequently, and no one was surprised.

Although the Second World War took its own toll on the houses – there were only eleven by the end of it – the task of keeping the paper going still set Dorothy on fire. Indeed, while many of the men were away at the front during the war, it was left to the women to maintain the journal.

What was the philosophy of this incredible woman? Amid all the millions of words she spawned, one passage stands out:

> Young people say, "What good can one person do?" They cannot see that we must lay one brick at a time; we can be responsible only for the one action at the present moment. But we can beg for an increase of love in our hearts that will vitalise and transform all our individual actions, and know that God will take them and multiply them, as Jesus multiplied the loaves and fishes.

Elsewhere she wrote: 'When we receive the Bread of Life each day, the grace we receive remains a dead weight in the soul unless we co-operate with the grace. When we co-operate with grace, we work with Christ in ministering to our brothers.'

Dorothy's final years were spent in constant activity as she made several speaking tours to India, Australia and Africa. In 1976, she made her last public appearance at the Eucharistic Congress in Pittsburgh. Soon afterwards, she had a heart attack and, although she continued to write until the end of her life and take her stint in the soup kitchen, she became less and less mobile. She died on the November 29 1980. Her beloved daughter, Tamar, was beside her; it was the quiet death for which she had wished.

Her funeral was attended by people from every state of the Union and further afield. As a Cardinal stepped forward to pronounce a blessing at the end, an intruder broke through the crowd, causing momentary panic among the dignitaries and security personnel. He gazed down at the coffin with unnerving intensity. No one stopped him. Perhaps he stood for all those strangers in whom Dorothy Day had seen the face of Christ.

CHRISTIAN DE CHERGE

Most Christians have heard the oft-quoted words attributed to St Francis of Assisi when he said 'preach the gospel everyday, sometimes use words.' The stories of the lives of the martyrs often fit into this category, of men and women who over the centuries have written the story of Christ in their blood. Most of us grew up hearing the stories of the early Church and the 'Christians being fed to the lions' – it is well documented even by pagan historians like Tacitus in the early second century. The persecution of the Church in Elizabethan times, during the French revolution and of course during our own Penal times are also well recorded. But many martyrs have died for the faith in the last century.

This month I want to remind ourselves of the silent witness of the Trappist martyrs of Algeria who died in 1996. Christians will recognise the beauty and values of the Islam faith but will also know that some people within that worldwide creed have distorted its principles and warped its ideals. Such a contrast to the suicide bomber is the one who gives his life for the sake of others.

'If it were ever to happen… that I should be the victim of the terrorism that seems to be engulfing all the foreigners now living in Algeria, I would like my community, my Church, my family to remember that my life was given to God and to this country.'

Fr Christian de Cherge, prior of a Trappist monastery in Algeria, began a letter with these words and sealed the envelope with these – 'to be opened in the event of my death.' The letter was indeed opened three years later after Christian and his fellow Trappists – seven men in all – had been killed by fundamentalist rebels in 1996. However, unlike many other Christian martyrs, these Trappists did not offer their lives for the conversion of their Muslim neighbours, but as a witness to the One God of all and for the cause of friendship among all God's people. For Fr Christian at least, it was the repayment of an ancient debt.

In 1958, when he was a young man of 21, he had served as a soldier fighting Algerian rebels in the brutal war of independence. One day his party were ambushed and his life was saved by a friend, who happened to be a devout Muslim. This man shielded him with his own body. This man's sacrifice, which Christian believed was prompted by religious faith, brought about his own conversion and eventually ordination to the priesthood and ultimately to the Trappist contemplative order. Christian studied in Rome and then asked to be assigned to a monastery dedicated to Our Lady in the Atlas mountains near Algiers. Many French religious had fled the country in the wake of the war, but at the urging of the archbishop, the Trappists had stayed on to offer a contemplative Christian presence among their Muslim neighbours.

The monks lived a traditional Trappist life of prayer and work, but they made a point of offering a place where Christians and Muslims could pray and talk together. A building in the monastery enclosure was offered for use as a mosque and so the 'sound of chapel bells mixed with the Muslim call to prayer.' This group was called 'Ribat el Salam' or the 'bond of peace'.

To many of their neighbours, they were trusted and respected – but to others the Trappists were foreign 'infidels'. As one dispatch put it: 'they live with the people and draw them away from the divine path, inciting them to follow the Gospel.' By 1993 the country was on the verge of anarchy and an ultimatum was given to all foreigners to leave the country, but the monks decided to stay. They also declined any military protection that was offered. It was at this time that Fr De Cherge wrote his last testament. The months progressed and several priests and women religious were killed. Still the monks remained.

'For us it is a journey of faith into the future and of sharing the present with our neighbours who have always been very closely bound to us. Now all that is left for us is to give our blood to follow Christ to the end.' That end came in 1996 on May 21 when rebels invaded the monastery compound and seized the monks and marched them into the mountains. A few weeks later a note was sent: 'we have slit the throats of the seven monks. Glory to God!' The heads were discovered the next day and they were buried in the small cemetery at the monastery.

De Cherge's family remembered his letter and opened it and discovered his prayer of forgiveness for his murderers:

'for me Islam and Algeria ... are body and soul.' Indeed Christian was so concerned that his eventual death might be a stumbling block to the dialogue he had helped to establish:

> I do not see how I could rejoice if this people I love were to be accused indiscriminately of my murder. It would be to pay too dearly for what will, perhaps be called "the grace of martyrdom", to owe it to an Algerian, whoever he may be, especially if he says he is acting in fidelity to what he believes to be Islam.

He offered thanks for all his friends and family. But he reserved his final words for his murderer:

> you too, my last minute friend, you who know not what you do. Yes, for you too I wish this thank you, and this adieu, which is of your planning. May we be granted to meet each other again, happy thieves, in paradise, should it please God, the Father of both of us. Amen! In sh'Allah !

CHARLES DE FOUCAULD

It is a shabby building. Outside broken bottles cover the ground. On the seventh floor, inside a modest apartment, is Tom who shares the place with two other men. It seems a typical 'bachelor pad' except for one thing: within the little space that they have there is a chapel and on an altar a small monstrance with the Sacred Host. Here is 'the heart for their journey'. What attracted you to the Little Brothers of Jesus?' one asks. 'I read something about Charles de Foucauld.'

Charles de Foucauld – born in 1858 in Strasbourg – might have been surprised at the response to his life some decades after his death. The young adult would not have given many indications of future sanctity. His childhood was marked by the tragedy of both parents' early deaths, whereafter maternal grandparents took custody of Charles and his sister.

In time, Charles entered the military academy, but he passed out low on the list of graduates because of his slovenliness and casual attitude. The substantial fortune that the grandfather had left to Charles proved his undoing, as he wasted the money on an extravagant lifestyle. Soon the academy dismissed him.

Charles then travelled to the North of Africa and used his exceptional linguistic skills to learn both Arabic and Hebrew. His journey through Morocco resulted in the publication of a book, *Reconnaissance de Maroc*, which received the gold medal of the Geographical Society of Paris.

By now Charles realised that Africa had changed him not just phys-ically – he had lost the weight of earlier years – but also spiritually. In Africa he had lived alongside two of the great monotheistic faiths and had admired their observance of regular prayer and the ethics of both the Torah and the Koran.

However, it was his exposure to the faith of this childhood as he saw it in the lives of people he met that moved him. Charles began to visit churches in France, voicing his agnostic prayer: 'My God, if you exist, make your existence known to me.'

Soon he was to meet Abbe Huvelin, a priest who lived a simple life instructing the many people who came to him. One of these was Charles, and soon he had made his confession and returned to the faith he had abandoned twelve years before. Huvelin persuaded Charles to visit the Holy Land in 1888.

He was overwhelmed by the sight of the places where Jesus had lived and preached. He would later write, 'I have lost my heart to this Jesus of Nazareth, crucified 1,900 years ago, and I spend my life trying to imitate him'.

Through the counsel of Abbe Huvelin, he entered a Trappist mon-astery in the Ardeche region of France on January 15 1890 and he received the habit on the Feast of Candlemas in 1891. Yet Charles wanted even more of the austerity for which the Trappists were re-nowned and he asked to move to a remote monastery in Syria.

There among the mountains he wrote, 'It moves you to compassion, for the poor, for workmen. You understand the cost of a piece of bread when you see the effort that goes to produce it'.

And yet nothing seemed to satisfy his spirit. He continued to lay his thoughts before Huvelin and by now these included the idea of founding his own religious order. During the winter of 1896/7, he was released from his vows and began to live the hidden life for which he yearned.

Charles returned to Nazareth and attached himself to a community of Poor Clares, working in the garden and doing basic tasks for them. By this time he had even allowed himself to study for the priesthood and he was ordained on June 9 1901. Still there was the idea within to form a group of men who would live a simple life but spend much time before the Blessed Sacrament.

A couple of years later, Charles received an invitation from an old military friend to go and work among the Tuareg people. Huvelin endorsed this plan, and in January 1904 he moved to this Saharan area. Charles wrote, 'I don't think there is any saying in the Gospel that has had a greater effect on me than this one: *whatever you do to one of these little ones you do to me*'.

The linguistic veracity Charles had already shown again came to the fore and he embarked on a translation of the gospels into the Tuareg language, an ancient language spoken even in Augustine's time. Charles settled in Tamanrasset, a village of about twenty families, and it was there he proposed to live his hidden life.

A mud hut was in time replaced with a stone one and Charles was at peace. Soon the nomads came to trust this spiritual 'nomad' and came to him for any medicines and food he had to spare. 'I want everybody – Christians, Muslims, Jews – to get used to seeing me as their brother. They are already beginning to call my house "the fraternity" and I like that.'

Three times Charles returned to France – 1908, 1911 and 1913 – each time hoping to persuade a companion to return with him. Each time he returned alone. By now his day was well regulated and organised as he divided it between work, sleep and prayer. He was beginning to write a rule for his new association whose members would live by the gospel, showing their friendship and vocation to love and respect members of other faiths.

The First World War began in 1914 and Charles could not escape it even in his isolation. The conflict between the European nations spilled over into the Saharan desert and touched the lives of the different tribes. Charles moved into a larger and better protected dwelling.

One night – December 1 1916 – he heard a voice outside and went to investigate. Immediately he was seized by a group of Senoussite tribesmen, who proceeded to pillage his dwelling.

A young boy with a rifle was left to guard Charles as all this happened. However, when two men appeared on camels, Charles tried to warn them and the boy panicked. His gun went off and a bullet went straight through Charles' head. He died instantly. A Muslim friend wrote to his sister: 'When I heard of the death of our friend, your brother Charles, my eyes closed. There was darkness all about me. I wept.'

The hidden life could not remain hidden for long, and a biography by Rene Bazin in 1921 inspired some young men to follow him. The first fraternity of the Little Brothers of Jesus was set up in 1933 on the edge of the Sahara, but it was not until after the Second World War that numbers began to flourish.

The brothers work alongside the poorest in the world, 'taking the lowest place', as Charles had done. Living in groups of two or three, Jesus in the Blessed Sacrament is their centre. Soon women too espoused the vocation, and the Little Sisters of Jesus were formed in the same spirit. On November 13 2005 Charles was beatified by Pope Benedict XVI.

Pier Giorgio Frassati

The adventurer, Chris Bonington, climbed mountains. No matter how high, or how terrible the conditions, he did not stop until he had conquered the peak before him. 'Why do you do it?' someone once asked. The reply was terse: 'Because it's there.'

Pier Giorgio Frassati was an avid skier and keen mountain climber, a man with film-star looks. Like Chris, he too could have said, 'because it's there'. Yet the real peak that Pier ascended was surely divine. 'On top of the mountains, I feel closer to God,' he once said. 'I leave my heart on the mountains, and if my studies permitted, I would spend whole days there, admiring the magnificence of God.'

Pier was born in Turin, in Italy, in April 1901, the son of Alfredo and Adelaide Frassati. His father was a senator in Italy and an ambassador to Germany, as well as being the founder of *La Stampa* magazine, which is still one of the most popular publications in Italy even today. In terms of class and social standing, Pier had everything.

However, although his parents raised him and his sister in the faith, they themselves were not particularly devout. It is true in every age, of course, that people pay lip service to God, never missing Mass or other major ceremonies, but seldom having prayer in the home, and never talking about their faith as a living reality. God is worshipped, but Jesus is never mentioned.

Pier's sister would later write, 'Our mother and her sister, who

would not have missed Sunday Mass or days of obligation for anything, were never seen by us to visit the Blessed Sacrament or go to
Benediction. They never went to communion, or were seen to kneel
and say a prayer'.

Despite this, Pier was a testimony to the miraculous way in which
God raises up in every generation men and women who help to re-
deem the age, who become the salt that has not lost its taste. This
athletic, outgoing and charming young man was also a daily commu-
nicant, at a time in the Church when that was not the norm.

When asked once why he performed so many acts of charity, Pier
replied, 'Jesus comes to visit me each morning in Holy Communion.
I return his visit to him in the poor.' Indeed, after every trip to the
mountains, he would immediately make a visit to the Blessed Sacrament in his local church.

The concern for the poor began at an early age. When he was four,
a poor woman appeared at the family door with a barefoot child in her
arms. Quickly, Pier stripped off his own socks and shoes, and handed
them over before anyone could question his actions. Another time, a
beggar came to the door, and his father sent him away cursorily. Pier
rushed to his mother, and the only way she could calm him down was
to tell him to run after the man and bring him back for some food.

When he was eighteen years of age, he enrolled in Turin's Royal
Polytechnic. He was planning a career in mining engineering, for he
felt that miners were among the most unfortunate of men in their
conditions and living standards. He could have chosen a life of ease,
but instead pursued a goal that reflected his concern for others and his
lack of interest in comfort and wealth.

In this same year, inspired by St Paul's discourse on love (1Cor. 13:
1-13), Pier joined the Society of St Vincent de Paul. This brought him
face to face with all manner of suffering but, as a friend later wrote, 'he
knew how to walk amid this lurid world's mud without getting dirty'.

Pier himself would say, 'As we grow close to the poor, bit by bit we gain their confidence, and can advise them in the most terrible moments of this earthly pilgrimage. We can give them the comforting words of faith, and we often succeed, not by our own merit, in putting on the right road people who have strayed without meaning to'.

Elsewhere he wrote: 'Don't ever forget that, even though the house is sordid, you are approaching Christ. Remember what the Lord said: "The good you do to the poor is good done to me". Around the sick, the poor, the unfortunate, I see a particular light that we do not have.'

Pier often had an eye for things that others ignored or did not notice. Once, when entering a club with some friends for a night out, he observed that the doorman was sad. The man's grandson had just died, and Pier offered him words of consolation and prayer. A year later, he was to remember the occasion and was able to renew his sympathy to the porter. Such kindness did not go amiss.

'From long-faced saints, deliver us, O Lord,' St Teresa of Avila once wrote. She would surely have approved of Pier Giorgio Frassati, for he certainly was not one of the sad saints. Right through his short life, he retained his friends, who knew him as a prankster and as a young man of robust and outgoing temperament. One friend nicknamed him 'Robespierre', and in his trips to the mountains he was never the one to hang back and wait for braver souls to venture forth.

In June 1925, Pier contracted polio while visiting an abandoned sick person. His grandmother was dying at the same time, and the family was so concerned for her health that no one really noticed the young man's deterioration. His mother, who tended to be over-critical at the best of times, could not understand why Pier was not present at his grandmother's final moments. By then, however, Pier was paralysed from the waist down. 'Pier Giorgio could choose a better moment to be ill,' she remarked coldly.

Even in his final hours, he was thinking of others. With one arm still functioning, spared from the paralysis that was creeping through him, he pulled a packet of medicine from his pocket with instructions regarding the poor person for whom it was intended. A few hours later he was dead. He was barely twenty-four years of age.

Once the news of his death got around, a remarkable thing happened. Within a short space of time, the doors began to open to let in a silent throng of people, unknown to his family. With faces blank or wet with tears, they went in to him to touch him like a relic.

His beloved poor, often living lives of quiet desperation, accompanied him for the final journey. His funeral was the first indication that his process of canonisation had begun. It was the poor of Turin, who knew their quiet visitor only as 'Fra Girolamo', who petitioned the Archbishop to begin the process which would eventually lead to his beatification.

In 1990, Pope John Paul declared Pier Giorgio blessed. The Pope said on that occasion:

> By his example, he proclaims that a life lived in Christ's spirit, the spirit of the Beatitudes, is blessed. He testifies that holiness is possible for everyone. He left this world rather young, but he made a mark upon this century, and not only on our century. In the Easter power of his baptism, he can say to everyone, especially to the young, "You will see me because I live, and you will live" (Jn. 14:19).

JOSEPH FREINADEMETZ

He was hard to escape though we weren't trying to avoid him! Everywhere we turned Joseph turned up. We saw his picture hanging in dining rooms and on beautiful mosaic tiles on cowbarns in the mountain villages. Even the very seminary where we stayed for a few nights – Bressanone in Alto Adige in Northern Italy – could stake a claim to him for he had been ordained within its walls. However, it was the Chinese who could most lay claim to Joseph or Shengfu Ruose, as they called him.

Centuries before Joseph, a Jesuit by the name of Matteo Ricci had gone as a missionary to the great land of China and had adopted Chinese customs and Chinese ways. He felt one had to become one with the people in order to tell them about Christ. Not everyone had understood Matteo's approach – especially at the level of the official Church – and his efforts did not bear the fruit he would have wanted. And yet the pictures we saw of Joseph were of a man who had adapted to the ways and the customs of this faraway nation.

The story of Joseph Freinademetz begins in the small town of Badia in the region of the Tyrol. When Joseph was born to Giovanmattia and Anna Maria, this region was in Austria but after the First World War it became part of Italy and so it remains. Joseph was born in 1852 and after seminary training was ordained in 1875. He took up duty in the community of San Martin de Tor, which was not far from his home.

Joseph would have been happy to remain there high up in the beautiful Tyrolese mountains, which lend themselves so much to the things of God. Certainly his parishioners appreciated his short ministry and would have wanted him to stay. But something was stirring in Joseph and when he heard of the new seminary for training missionaries in Steyl in Holland, he was determined to go.

Fr Arnold Janssen was the founder of this new missionary organisation, The Divine Word Missionaries, and Joseph was eager to join him and the other members of this fledgling community. A few years of training and one brief visit home and in 1879 Joseph set off for China with another priest, John Baptist Anzer, later to be made bishop. He would never return home again.

Those early years were tough – long journeys, assaults by bandits and the often difficult work of forming and establishing the first Christian communities. When they arrived in the province of Shantung, there were 158 Christians out of a population of over 12 million. It was truly missionary work. Joseph realised quickly that if the seeds planted were to bear fruit and the communities were not to die, they had to have a committed laity and especially catechists. He gave a lot of time and energy to producing a manual in Chinese that would help his laity to pass on the faith to their new converts. This task could not have been easy, given the difficulty of learning the Chinese language, but right from the start Joseph's life was marked by a desire to become more like a Chinese man among the Chinese. In a letter home he had written 'I love China and the Chinese; I want to die among them and be laid to rest among them.' Indeed when one sees pictures of Joseph he does indeed look more Chinese than European.

Along with the other Divine Word Missionaries, Joseph realised the need for local people to be involved in the work of their own Church. He put great energy into the formation of Chinese priests and served at a time as rector of the seminary and later spiritual director. He always exercised his authority in a brotherly way and the respect he received from this gracious people witnessed to his own example and life.

The basis of all of this apostolic effort was his own life of prayer: 'Do you imagine you can become holy without meditation, something no saint was able to do? Without meditation life is lost.' He said his daily Mass and prayed the divine office with the same intense dedication he did his other missionary work.

In 1898, came the beginning of his struggle with tuberculosis. A sore throat did not go away and soon developed into the disease that so ravaged whole continents at the beginning of the 20th century. The bishop recommended some time away and Joseph duly went to Japan for a while to rest. He quickly returned to be present in the diocese when The Boxer rebellion against all things European threatened the work of decades among the Chinese. The German authorities had even ordered all missionaries to leave for their own safety, but Joseph remained on, knowing full well the risk he was taking. Indeed two young Divine Word priests lost their lives at this difficult time.

Joseph survived that period in Chinese history, but the selfless years were taking their toll. Often when the bishop left the diocese, he was the one who took over administration. Once when there was an outbreak of typhus, he went like a good shepherd to the area most affected in order to offer assistance. Sadly he became infected and within a short time died, on January 28 2008. He was buried at the twelfth station on the Way of the Cross at Taikia, South Shandong, and soon his grave became a site of pilgrimage for Chinese Christians.

Along with Arnold Janssen and Daniel Comboni, Fr Joseph was canonised by Pope John Paul On October 5 2003. The man from the other side of the world, the Sud Tyrol, had become a Chinese saint. His life was an expression of his motto: 'the language that all people understand is that of love.'

BILLY GRAHAM

The face of Billy Graham was probably one of the best known of the second half of the 20th century. He was associated with Bible-based Christianity, and was capable of filling big stadiums with people who wanted to hear his stirring message. Through the decades, Graham became chaplain, as it were, to the American nation, and confidante of virtually every President from Eisenhower to Clinton.

The story of Billy Graham has humble beginnings, however. He was born on a farm in Charlotte, North Carolina, on November 7 1918, the eldest of four children, to parents who were of 'God-fearing, Scottish Presbyterian stock'.

Billy was not particularly religious in his early youth. His farther knew that, at that stage in his life, he accompanied the family to church each week 'grudgingly or out of necessity'. Things were to change, however, when Billy heard the preaching of a visiting evangelist, Mordecai Ham.

'His words grabbed my mind and gripped my heart,' he would later claim. 'What was slowly dawning on me during those weeks, was the miserable realisation that I did not know Jesus Christ for myself. I could not depend on my parents' faith. Faith could not be passed on as an inheritance, like the family silver. It had to be exercised by each individual.'

And so, one night, after the sermon, Billy decided to put himself forward and commit himself to Christ. As he did so, the soloist led the congregation in the song *Just as I am*. This was the title Graham was to use many years later for his own autobiography. About that occasion he wrote, 'No bells went off inside me. No signs across the ceiling. I simply felt at peace.'

By the time he was eighteen, Billy felt called to full-time ministry. He pursued that aim by attending college, and then the Florida Bible Institute, from 1937–40. The latter helped to broaden his view of the Church and, although his exposure was still only to evangelical Christianity, it served as a basis for that later openness and ecumenical spirit which have marked Graham's ministry through the decades.

One night in 1938, during his evening walk of a local golf course, Billy made a commitment to full-time service of the Lord. The following year he was ordained a Baptist minister. 'I read *Ephesians* again and again,' he later wrote, 'where it mentions that the Lord gave some to be evangelists and some to be pastors. God just did not want me to be a pastor. It was time to take up what the Lord called me to do – evangelism.'

The apostolate of evangelism in huge stadiums and civic centres across the globe did not begin immediately. He preached wherever he was invited. In this way, as well as begin a youth ministry, he came to host a Christian radio show: 'Youth for Christ'. Graham and others organised Saturday night youth rallies in several cities, drawing large crowds.

Gradually, a pattern developed. Billy and his team of able workers would arrive in a town or city. A hall or large tent would be booked, and there the team would set up base. A rally would begin with several gospel songs, and then Billy would preach, concluding always by inviting people to come forward to accept Christ as their Lord and Saviour. It is with this 'altarcall' that many have come to associate the name of Billy Graham.

There were two key features of these rallies, however, that were important and that never varied over the years. The first was that Billy always enlisted a small army of people to pray for the ministry. These forty or fifty people sat together in front of the stage or platform, with 'their faces full of expectant faith that God was about to work again'.

Secondly, Graham was no evangelical 'sheep-stealer'. Prior to arriving in a city or country, he would enlist the support of the local clergy, and it was to these that the people who responded to the 'altar call' were referred for follow-up. He well knew that many who might respond to the Spirit's prompting at a rally needed local support in order to grow and be sustained. Among those he contacted were local Catholic priests.

Graham's message was simple and direct, varying little from place to place and rally to rally. 'I have had the privilege of preaching the gospel on every continent in most of the countries of the world. And I have found that when I present the simple message of the gospel of Jesus Christ with authority, quoting from the very Word of God, he takes that message and drives it supernaturally into the human heart.'

Although Billy Graham came from a typical Southern Baptist background, which traditionally had not been sympathetic to Catholicism, he has broken that mould. Billy has always respected people for what they are. Consequently, it comes as no surprise that he had a great respect for Pope John Paul II.

Their contact began in 1978, when Cardinal Wojtyla invited Graham to preach in Krakow cathedral. They didn't actually meet on that occasion, however. Pope John Paul I had died suddenly, and the Cardinal had to leave for Rome and the consistory, which would eventually elect him to the See of Peter. Graham preached also at the great Marian shrine of Czestochowa, and is on record as being deeply impressed by the faith of Catholic Poland.

Three years later, Billy did indeed meet the Pope, this time in Rome.

He found him extremely cordial and very interested in his ministry. 'After only a few minutes,' he wrote, 'I felt as if we had known each other for many years.' The two men of God exchanged gifts. Graham gave the Pope a woodcarving of a shepherd with his sheep, crafted by a North Carolina artist.

They recalled together the words of Jesus: 'I am the Good Shepherd; I know my own and my sheep know me... There are other sheep I have that are not of this fold, and I must lead these too' (Jn. 10: 14-16). In turn, the Pope gave Graham a medallion of his papacy and several beautifully bound volumes.

There was another great Catholic leader to whom Billy had a strong affinity, not least because they shared a common zeal for God's Word and because both were blessed by God with the skills of oratory. Fulton Sheen, now deceased, was Bishop of Rochester in his time, but was more known throughout America as one of the earliest 'televangelists'.

Graham recalled the first time they met. He wrote:

One night on a train from Washington to New York, I was just drifting off to sleep when a knock came on my apartment door. I was too tired to answer it. In daytime, I would have happily obliged, but this was the middle of the night. The knocker persisted. I finally unlocked the compartment door and opened it a crack. There, greeting me, was one of the most familiar faces in America, not just to Roman Catholics, but to everyone else. It was Bishop Sheen.

"Billy, I know it is late, but may I come in for a chat and a prayer?" I was in my pyjamas, but I was delighted to see him and invited him in. We talked about our ministries and our common commitment to evangelism, and I told him how grateful I was for his ministry and his focus on Christ. We talked further and we prayed; and by the time he left I felt as if I had known him all my life. We became good friends.

Billy was all too easily aware of another accusation that was sometimes made: that his message was all too much 'pie in the sky'. Yet he believed that the gospel was a word for a broken world. In a 1952 crusade in Jackson, Mississippi, ropes had been put up to segregate blacks and whites. Billy physically took the ropes down, saying, 'we're all equal before God'. He did not allow them to be put up again.

So what was Billy Graham about? What had he been about for fifty years around the world? Above all, it was a yearning for people to hear the message of Christ, and to accept it as their own. Billy would claim that:

> people are searching for something today, and if they don't believe in God they must have a substitute for God. Among young people there is a great identity crisis today. Who am I? What is the purpose of life? Where did I come from? Where am I going? The Bible has a direct answer to these great questions, and unless God seals the vacuum in people, and especially the young today, then some other ideology will, because people must believe in something to find fulfilment in their lives.

DOLORES HART

'What was it like kissing Elvis?' she once was asked. She chuckled a bit at the memory. 'I think the limit for a screen kiss was 15 seconds then. That one has lasted forty years!' Even after all that time she still enjoyed the conversation.

Not many nuns could claim that they starred in a film with Elvis Presley or could count Stephen Boyd, Robert Wagner and George Hamilton among their friends. Stars of yesterday they may be, but in their time they were the big names of Hollywood – akin to Brad Pitt or George Clooney or Colin Farrell of today.

Dolores Hicks (stage name Hart) was born in 1938, an only child to an actor, Bert Hicks, and Harriet his wife. Sadly they separated when she was three but in those early years Bert had introduced her to the Hollywood life and to Beverley Hills. 'I always wanted to be part of that life' Dolores would later admit. As a child she used to enjoy watching the films in the local cinema with her grandfather, who was a projectionist. Dolores would watch the films again and again, sometimes without sound so as not to disturb her grandfather, who often took a nap in the booth! It gave her a taste for the life to come.

After school Dolores moved into the movie world herself and she took on the stage name of 'Dolores Hart'. In 1956 she was the love interest for Elvis in a film called *Loving You* and this led to other starring roles before working with Presley again in 'King Creole' (1958). Dolores always denied ever having an intimate relationship with Presley, but she sometimes took a sort of mischievous delight in responding to the question with which I began these thoughts.

There were other roles and awards and nominations from the world of Broadway. 1960 saw her star in a film *Where the Boys Are*, which became a very popular hit with so many because it dealt with the issues of sexuality and popularity, which were beginning to appear in films of the time. In 1961 she starred in the film *Francis of Assisi*, in which she played the part of Clare, the friend of the great saint. While she was filming in Rome she met Pope John XXIII and she told him who she was and who she was playing. The Pontiff replied very emphatically – and perhaps prophetically – '*Tu sei Chiara*' (you are Clare).

There were four more films to follow including a role opposite Hugh O'Brien in 1963 in *Come Fly with Me*. But then at the height of her career, she stunned the world by making the decision to become a cloistered nun and enter the Benedictine monastery of Regina Laudis. 'I just knew that this was what God wanted for me,' she said years later, 'and yet I never felt I was walking away from Hollywood. I felt I was walking into something more significant and by that I took Hollywood with me.'

'Star Driven into Nunnery by her Love for Elvis' was one of the media headlines at the time, but Dolores said it wasn't like that at all. Indeed at the beginning when an excited producer mentioned that she would be starring in a film with Elvis, she innocently asked: 'Oh, what does he do?'

She might not have fallen in love with Elvis, but she was a vivacious young woman to whom men were drawn. More than one actor had less than pure intentions, but she never let herself be compromised. When she did accept the marriage proposal of Don Robinson, her longtime boyfriend, her grandmother told her 'don't marry a man because you want to live with him – marry him because you can't live without him.' It turned out that the man she could not live without was Jesus. Even Don knew that. With the invitations printed, the dress fittings done, at an engagement party he said to her – 'your heart isn't here. Go back to Regina Laudis and figure it out.'

Yet the transition was not as smooth as Dolores might have reflected years later. As a novice in the Abbey, she told the Abbess: 'I will never have to worry again about being an actress, because it was all over and behind me.' Abbess Benedict replied 'I'm sorry, but you are completely wrong. Now you have to take up a role and really work at it.'

Dolores 'disappeared' into the monastic life, taking the name Sister Judith initially, but changed it back to her own name at final vows, which she took in 1970. There she has remained with her community who pray the office eight times each day and who run a farm of 400 acres. There has been no 'leaping back over the convent wall'. However, through the years Dolores was able to maintain her links with Hollywood. Actors like Paul Newman have helped her raise money to pay for lighting and staging for the abbey's own theatre and every Summer for the last few years the community has put on a musical – *West Side Story* and *Fiddler on the Roof* being just two examples.

Dolores has been prioress of the abbey since 2001 but she also remains a member of the Academy of Motion Picture Arts and Sciences, thus being the only nun to be an Oscar voting member.

She has also shown how film can be an artistic medium for spiritual growth, and by filming the community's activities over the years she has provided an invaluable insight into the contemplative life.

Dolores was to attend the great Oscar event just once more – in 2012, the first time since 1959 when she had been a Hollywood starlet. The occasion was the nomination for the best documentary award. She herself was the 'star' but the title of the film said it all – *God is the Bigger Elvis*.

ROSE HAWTHORNE

My little sister died last May – in the Trinity hospice in Blackpool. The first warning signs came the previous September. As my brother said it is not good when you hear the words 'cancer' and 'rare' in the same sentence. From that early diagnosis to the end she fought hard. She underwent the treatments – she found the chemo tough, but never complained. To the end she was smiling and brave and asking about others. Her faithful husband was with her every step of the way. Her brothers – all four of us – made frequent trips across the Irish Sea as often as our lives and schedules allowed. Five days before she died I celebrated Mass in her bedroom surrounded by her four 'Musketeers' and their wives and Anne's husband and children. It was an emotional occasion. I could not preach but the sign of peace we all gave that day said a thousand words.

When it was all over and Anne was buried and we all returned to pick up the pieces of our lives I found time to drop a note of thanks to the Hospice. I had been in hospices before and did not feel ill at ease in their quiet surroundings. But Trinity had been special – maybe because this time it was personal. I thanked them for their quiet presence and their comfort and support. Everything was right for the moment.

I don't suppose any of us who enter a hospice to visit a relative or to minister as I often have to do think about the origins of the hospice movement. Though she is little acknowledged as a founder, the name of Rose Hawthorne is prominent in helping people to think differently about death and dying. Rose was an American who was born in May 1851, the third child of the author Nathaniel Hawthorne. Her early years were actually spent in Liverpool where her father was US consul. Something of her father's talent for writing had passed on to Rose, and soon she too was writing regularly for magazines and periodicals. Sadly, her father died early in her life – she was but thirteen – and her mother followed soon afterwards.

This early experience of death did not prepare her well for marriage. Perhaps to an extent she 'fell' into the arms of George Lathrop, a young American writer whom she had met in Europe. He was a good 'catch'. A child was born but soon tragedy followed – the boy died sadly at four, and George's alcoholism was driving a wedge between them until eventual separation. Despite the fact that they had both converted to Catholicism in 1891, the marriage ended just two years later.

Rose found herself now in her forties and seemingly without direction – up to then her life had been spent in honest devotion to her husband but also in the frivolous pursuits of 'society' and in the salons of New York. Something was missing. It is hard to believe it now but at one time cancer was considered much in the same way as people once saw leprosy. Indeed, once diagnosed, cases of cancer were not permitted to remain in New York hospitals. Those without family or means were banished to die in bleak isolation on Blackwell's Island. A priest told Rose of one particular case, where a young seamstress, a sensitive woman, had developed cancer. She was thrown out of her room and spent all her savings in the hopeless search for a cure. A private hospital sent her to the city hospital and they packed her off to a poor house on Blackwell Island. Rose was beginning to see her vocation.

Initially she undertook a course in nursing and then found lodging in one of the poorest quarters in the city, on the Lower East side. First she set about visiting the cancer patients in their own homes, but very soon she was inviting them to her own apartment where she nursed them until they died. For support she relied on the gifts and financial contributions that her friends and others gave. For a woman of refined taste it was a big change. Day after day she dressed the wounds and cleaned the sores of the sick. She tended to their bedsores, but above all she was determined not just to provide a physical need, but also to show friendship and respect to those who had become outcasts.

In 1900 Rose felt that she should formalise the work she was doing and with a dear friend, Alice Huber, entered religious life in the form of the Dominican order. Six years later her own religious order was formed, the Servants of Relief for Incurable Cancer, and Rose became known as Mother Alphonsa. Their work continued until early in the 21st century, when it closed due to the increased availability of adequate public and private treatment.

Rose herself died in 1926 and her case for canonisation is well begun. Fr George O'Donnell, her postulator, wrote:

> Service to Christ's poor did not simply mean that this lady of culture and social status would put on an apron and offer gifts from her abundance. She decided to live among the poor, to beg for them as they did for themselves, and to establish a home where they could live in dignity as they faced their final lives on earth. There was to be no class system, no 'upstairs/ downstairs' for her residents. She and her religious sisters would be the servant. Rose saw in men and women suffering from cancer the face of Christ.

Today we take for granted the calming presence of the 'hospice' in every major town or city. They are there to give peace to those whose lives are drawing to a close. They are there for those who are trying to come to terms with the passing of a loved one. I remain grateful for the dignity with which my sister died. I am grateful for Trinity – and for Rose.

MADELEINE HUTIN

There is a statue in Rome called 'The Ecstasy of St Teresa', which captures a moment in the life of the Spanish mystic when she seems consumed totally by the overwhelming love of God. 'You have seduced me Lord, and I have let myself be seduced' Jeremiah would write, in chapter 20 of his prophetic work.

Madeleine Hutin was one such young woman, who felt such a passion for Jesus that she felt no religious congregation at the time in France could satisfy her longing. Then in her twenties – and very much with the wise guidance of her saintly father – she came across a biography of the French priest Charles de Foucauld who had died in the Sahara desert in 1916.

Charles had envisioned a new style of contemplative life, which was rooted in the poor and based on the 'hidden years' of Jesus. In his hermitage in the desert he had conceived a fraternity of men and women who would live among their Muslim neighbours as brothers and sisters with a spirit of prayer and manual labour. In this way they would proclaim the gospel not with words but with their lives. For many years, Foucauld had patiently waited for followers to come, but in the end he died alone. It was left to others like Madeleine to embrace the vision and to bring it to fruition.

Poor health prevented Madeleine putting her dream into operation initially and she was not able to do anything until she was thirty-eight.

Then in 1936 she set sail for Algiers, trusting in Providence to give her what she needed and to give her direction for the life ahead. Soon she was introduced to Fr Rene Voillaume who himself had been converted by the same biography of Foucauld, and who had initiated the Little brothers of Jesus who had been living in the desert from 1933. Rene listened very attentively to the young woman, and felt that she could bring this new charism and vocation to the vision of women. Soon the Little Sisters of Jesus had begun and it was established under the direction and leadership of Madeleine.

The word 'little' had special meaning for Madeleine just as the hidden and anonymous life of Christ had meaning for Charles de Foucauld. During the early years of her vocation, she was inspired by her reflection on the infant Jesus. The humility, weakness and vulnerability of a baby were the disguises in which the savior of the world had come among men. It seemed so appropriate to her that this baby should also be the inspiration and model for those who wished to bear witness to the love of God among the poorest and weakest of society. Theirs was not the vocation to come with money and resources to help others. Their vocation was to be truly *'Emanuel'* – 'God with us'.

Anyone who has ever read the history of any religious order will know that it can take years before the order or congregation is recognised. Somewhere along the line, the vision of the founder is misunderstood or misinterpreted. Even the great St Francis suffered this humiliation. It was no less the case for Madeleine and her original sisters. It took years before the order was recognised by Rome and along the way there were doubts and criticisms and deviations from her original vision.

After all it was a new style of religious life. They were neither contemplative nor were they engaged in traditional apostolic activities. The sisters lived in small fraternities, sometimes no more than two or three in a house. While maintaining an intense commitment to contemplative prayer, they also tried to enter fully into the life and culture of the local community. Instead of a traditional habit they wore a simple denim garb adorned with a cross and they shared the local food and livelihood of those who lived around them. Madeleine had written 'the world looks for efficiency more than for the unobtrusive-ness of the hidden life. Bethlehem and Nazareth will always remain a mystery to it.'

At the beginning Madeleine conceived of a mission among the Muslims of North Africa – indeed it was there that the congregation took root and flourished. Yet by the time of her death in 1989, the numbers of sisters had grown to over 1,400 and these could be found in 280 communities all over the world. Wherever there was poverty of spirit and a need the sisters were there. From sisters who travelled with gipsy caravans to those who lived in the slums of London or Beirut, from remote Eskimo villages to the boat people of South East Asia – in so many diverse places the sisters lived and worked and prayed. Whatever the setting, the aim of the Little Sisters was not to evange-lise in a formal sense but to serve modestly as a kind of leaven in the midst of the world with a spirit of love.

In 1949, Madeleine formally gave up her role as leader of the con-gregation preferring to play a role as mother to the sisters in the vari-ous parts of the world. Despite the frailty of her early years, she con-tinued to enjoy good health right up to the end and never shirked the demands and rigours of each community wherein she found herself. It was during one final exhausting trip to the Soviet Union in 1989 that she succumbed to her age and frailty. Her funeral and farewell Mass took place at the Rome Centre Tre Fontane on November 10 1989, the day the Berlin wall came down. It was a fitting testament to a woman who broke down walls all her life.

FRANZ JAGERSTATTER

No account of the martyrs of the Nazi era can leave out the remarkable story of the Austrian Franz Jagerstatter. His story is both simple and complex. He was born to an unmarried farmer's maid in 1907 in a village called St Radegund in Western Austria. His mother later married Herr Jagerstatter, who adopted the young boy.

As a teenager, Franz gained a reputation as a rather wild young man. He always showed a streak of courage – in the end it cost him his life. But in those early days he would have fought with the village gang against rivals from other villages. He was indeed a drinker, a brawler and a bit of a womaniser.

Yet when he was twenty, he left the village to work in the salt mines some distance away, and when he returned about three years later, he had acquired two things: a motor cycle, the first in the village; and a religious faith that made him as pious as before he was wild. The villagers could scarcely believe it was the same person. He even thought of becoming a priest, but the parish priest advised against this, saying that his parents needed him to take over the farm. And this is what he did.

In 1936 he married Francesca, a girl also of deep religious faith, and the pair honeymooned in Rome where they received a blessing from the Pope at a general audience. On his return, Franz settled down to a typical peasant life. He rose very early and worked on the farm, often being heard singing to the cows as he milked them and saying the rosary as he ploughed.

Often he would forego even his breakfast in order to be able to receive Holy Communion, the regular reception of which was not a practice at this time. In addition to his farm and household duties he became sexton of the local parish church and become known for his diligent service.

However Franz did not close his eyes to what was happening in the world outside the farm. He believed the Nazis were evil and their wars were unjust. He became known for his opposition to the Nazi regime, casting the only local vote out of over 500 against the Anschluss (the annexation of Austria by Germany in 1938).

Around that year, he wrote to a friend: 'Since the death of Christ, almost every century has seen the persecution of Christians; there have always been heroes and martyrs who gave their lives for Christ and their faith. We too, must become heroes of the faith.'

In the meantime, he went about his business, much like others, but with important differences. He had three children and a farm to run, but Franz did not use family needs as an excuse to deviate in the slightest from what was right. He stopped going to taverns, not because he was a teetotaller, but because he got into fights over Nazism.

At the same time, he practised charity to the poor in the village, though he was only a little better than poor himself. The usual custom in the village was to give a donation to the church sexton for his help in arranging funerals and prayer services. Franz refused this, preferring to join with the faithful rather than act as a paid official. The period of self-discipline prepared him for much more demanding sacrifices.

As the Nazis organised Austria, Jagerstatter had to decide whether to allow himself to be drafted by the German army and thus collaborate with Nazism. When Franz was called to active duty in the military, he sought advice from at least three priests and a bishop.

Each appealed to his conscience to assure him that this service was consistent with his Christianity.

First, he was told, he had to consider his family. The other argument was that he had a responsibility to obey legitimate authorities. The political authorities were the ones liable to judgment for their decisions, not ordinary citizens. Franz rejected both arguments. To the core, Franz recoiled at any sense of lies, and so he refused to serve. The consequences of Jagerstatter's position were obvious: 'Everyone tells me, of course, that I should not do what I am doing because of the danger of death. I believe it is better to sacrifice one's life right away than to place oneself in the grave danger of committing sin and then dying.' Franz was clear he could change nothing in world affairs, but he wished 'to be at least a sign that not everyone let themselves be carried away with the tide. Francesca, his wife, initially objected to his stance but in the end supported him. 'If I had not stood by him he would have had no one,' she said.

Jagerstatter was sent to the prison in Linz, where Hitler and Eichmann had lived as children. His Way of the Cross would not be long. In May, he was transferred to a prison in Berlin. On August 9 1943, he accepted execution, even though he knew it would make no earthly difference to the Nazi death machine. He and fifteen others were guillotined and forced to lie face-up without a blindfold to watch the blade come down.

Some three years later his ashes were taken back to his village and buried by the church wall in St Radegund where his wife was sacristan for many years after him.

A Father Jochmann was the prison chaplain in Berlin, and spent some time with Jagerstatter that day. He reports that the prisoner was calm and uncomplaining. He refused any religious material, even a New Testament, because, he said, 'I am completely bound in inner union with the Lord, and any reading would only interrupt my communication with my God'. Father Jochmann later said of him, 'I can say with certainty that this simple man is the only saint I have ever met in my lifetime.'

On June 1 2007, Pope Benedict XVI issued a decree recognising Franz Jagerstatter as a martyr. This meant that his beatification process would begin immediately and he should be declared Blessed in the not too-distant future.

Jerome Lejeune

Niall is one of my altar boys. He holds the missal for me at the time of the special prayers – the Collect and Post Communion – at the start and end of Mass. Sometimes he will sneak a little 'smirk' at me before I get all solemn and pray! He also loves to ring the bell, though he doesn't always get his timing right! He fits in so well with the other boys at the Sunday 12.00 Mass – I call them the 'A-Team'!

Sometimes I banter with Niall and joke about his bald patch. I am not one to joke in this regard! He gives as good as he gets. When Liverpool are playing he confidently predicts the score and reminds me of it loudly when it comes true. Niall really is a special altar boy, all forty-one years of him!

Last Monday I celebrated a requiem Mass for a lovely old lady who passed away at the age of 92 after a relatively short illness. Despite early poverty and difficult circumstances she had lived life to the full, had reared six children and saw plenty of the next generations too. She had much to be proud of but above all there was her untiring devotion and care of her 'special son' Damien. He was the youngest. 'So long as Damien was all right, Sarah was all right.' And Damien needed and needs more attentive care than my altar boy Niall.

I mention these little stories because of the man I want to honour this month. Jerome Lejeune was a French geneticist who is credited with discovering the chromosome abnormality in humans that causes Downs Syndrome. He was born in Montrouge (Hauts-de-Seine) in France in 1926 and after his basic medical education at the Paris School of Medicine he went on to specialise in pediatrics and genetics. He worked mainly at the French National Centre for Scientific Research. In time he married Birthe Bringsted and they had five children, two sons and three daughters. At the time of Jerome's death in 1994 the couple had been married 42 years.

It was in 1958 that Lejeune was working in the laboratory with two colleagues, Raymond Turpin and Marthe Gautier. There has been some dispute about who exactly made the discovery, but their findings were published by the French Academy of Sciences. The trio found that a defect in intellectual development was shown to be linked to chromosomal abnormalities.

As Lejeune and Gautier studied the hands of children with Downs Syndrome, they deduced that their dermatoglyphic (the fingerprints and lines on their hands) anomalies appeared during embryo formation. They showed for the first time that there were 47 chromosomes in a child with Downs Syndrome, as compared to the 46 that had been discovered just a short time before in the human species.

Downs had in fact been known for about a hundred years before, but it was Lejeune's focused research which discovered the link with chromosomes which are microscopically small bodies located in the nuclei of cells of animals and plants. A fellow scientist said that Lejeune's discovery 'basically opened up the whole scientific field of genetic disorders. After his discovery, he became a prominent advocate of humane care for people with Downs Syndrome, and attempted to use his findings and the findings of others to help. He would have been horrified that discovery of the genetic disorder would in time lead to many people deciding to abort their Downs baby and other fetuses with chromosome abnormalities. As a Catholic he found this distressing.

Birthe, Jerome's wife of 42 years said of her husband that he was a devout Catholic, but discreet about it. He prayed often but quietly and did not boast about his faith. She also said that he never won the Nobel Prize probably because of his opposition to abortion, and this did not sit well with certain people in the world of science. After receiving one specific prize for medical research, he gave a talk, which questioned the morality of abortion. In a letter to his wife who was not present he wrote: 'Today I lost my Nobel Prize in Medicine.'

Jerome also knew Pope John Paul even before the latter became Pope. Indeed they had lunch together on May 13 1981, the very day that Mehemet Ali Acqa tried to assassinate John Paul in St Peter's Square, while the Papal car was circling the pilgrims. Karol Wojtyla, as archbishop of Krakow, had met Lejeune through a mutual friend, Dr Wanda Poltawska, who had asked him to speak at conferences. In time Lejeune, would be invited by the Pope to lead a new Pontifical academy for Life, which was very dear to his heart. Lejeune drafted the laws and oaths that each member of the academy would later take.

Sadly Jerome was diagnosed with lung cancer in November 1993. He served as President of the academy only a few weeks before his death in April 1994. Pope John Paul would later visit his grave, prior to the world Youth Day in Paris in 1997. Already Lejeune has been named a 'servant of God' by the Church, and his cause for sainthood is well advanced.

When I think of Sarah and her Damien, as well as Niall and his widowed mother, I am filled with total admiration for their love and dedication, for the way that they have been able to say 'yes' so completely. They teach me how to love.

Some years ago I attended a Charismatic open air rally. I was one of the speakers. During the lively songs all of us saw a group of Downs young adults doing the Conga through the crowd. We all wanted to join in and give play to our emotions for the Lord, but 'self-respect' prevented many of us from doing so. Only those young adults were really free. Sometimes I wonder who has the handicap!

CS LEWIS

'God whispers to us in our pleasures; He speaks to us in our silence and He shouts to us in our pain.' The words rolled eloquently and confidently off his tongue as he spoke to yet another eager group of ladies from the Women's Institute. The film 'Shadowlands' (1993) captured this and other moments so graphically in its portrayal of the speaker.

Clive Staples Lewis, affectionately known as 'Jack' to his friends, died fifty years ago this month. He was indeed the successor to Justin and Augustine for the 20th century. He was the Apologist to explain the Christian faith to a godless age, which had come through the Great Depression and emerged from a horrific war, which took the lives of over fifty million people. 'Where was God in all this?' many would ask, and Lewis tried to answer their questions. And yet his certainties would be tested later in his own life when late romance blossomed, only to be snatched from him after a few short years. About that later.

Lewis was born in Belfast in November 1898, his father a prominent barrister and his mother a teacher and mathematician. School was not a pleasant experience for the young Clive as he moved from one boarding location to another. However his undoubted intelligence shone through and in 1917 he entered University College in Oxford. By this time, he had long lost his faith, though the loss of his mother when he was ten did not help him adjust readily to adult life and values.

In 1917 he also entered the war and experienced trench warfare in the area of the Somme in Northern France. The following April he was wounded in battle though two of his colleagues were killed in the same 'friendly' fire of a British shell, which fell short of its target. Recovery and depression followed before he was demobilised at the end of 1918.

The years that followed were full of productivity as he established himself as a scholar and then lecturer and then later as professor of Mediaeval and Renaissance literature at Cambridge. Various scholarly works emerged in the late 1930s and early 40s. With his brother Warren, their house was the archetypal bachelors' residence and Lewis was more than happy with this arrangement. The Catholic writer JRR Tolkien of *The Lord of the Rings* fame was in Lewis' close circle of friends.

The journey back to faith was a gradual one. Lewis had as a teenager echoed the Roman poet Lucretius in an argument for atheism:

'Had God designed the world, it would not be a world so frail and faulty as we see.'

Religion had seemed a chore and a duty, but yet he described himself as 'being angry at God for not existing!' In the end God had His way, as Lewis described in *Surprised by Joy*:

> You must picture me alone in that room in Magdalen, night after night, feeling whenever my mind lifted even for a second from my work, the steady unrelenting approach of Him whom I so earnestly desired not to meet. That which I greatly feared had at last come upon me. In the Trinity term of 1929 I gave in and admitted that God was God and knelt and prayed; perhaps that night the most dejected and reluctant convert in all England.

After this initial conversion to theism, Lewis converted to Christianity and later reentered the Anglican Communion with his brother Warren in 1931.

This moment in his life led to another great explosion of creativity and writing as Lewis began a second phase of writing. There flowed from his prolific pen a whole host of Christian apologetic texts, which are as much loved today as they were when first written – *The Problem of Pain*, *The Screwtape Letters*, *Mere Christianity*, *Miracles*, *The Four Loves*, and many others. Karol Wojtyla – for one – used to love to bring *The Screwtape Letters* with him on his kayaking trips with young people into the Tatra mountains in Poland.

In addition to all these more serious excursions, there was also the seven part series written for children *The Chronicles of Narnia* with its Christ-figure in the shape of Aslan the lion. Along with *The Lion, the Witch and the Wardrobe*, these beautiful stories have been made popular for both the small screen and the cinema, thus bringing them to a new generation of people and children. It is estimated that in the last few decades these books have sold over 100 million copies in over 40 different languages.

Yet even for someone with rekindled faith and a vocabulary and mind to defend it, there was a testing. Romance blossomed late in Clive's life – in 1956 he married the American writer Joy Davidman, who was seventeen years his junior. They were blissfully happy and Lewis could never have guessed that his bachelorhood would ever have come to an end. Yet, tragically, Joy developed cancer and died after but four years of marriage. The words about God shouting to us in our pain became all too real for a grieving Lewis, whose faith was sorely tested by this event. Again the lovely film *Shadowlands* starring Anthony Hopkins and Debra Winger captured admirably the struggle of faith that engulfed Lewis after his wife's death. Somehow he survived although he himself was only to last another three years himself.

At the time his death on November 22 1963 passed almost unnoticed as it occurred on the same day as President Kennedy's assassination. The press was caught up with 'conspiracies' and bigger events, but in 2013 – on his 50th anniversary – Lewis was honoured with a memorial in Poet's Corner in Westminster Abbey. His deep scholarship, clarity and sharp wit made him perhaps the most effective and persuasive Christian apologist of the 20th century.

ANTON LULI

The old Jesuit can hardly walk, but when he gets to the Pope, he starts to go down on his knees to kiss the Pope's ring. But the Pope grabs him by the shoulders and starts to haul him up. It seemed as if the Pope was not going to let this man bow to him after all he had been through. Forty-two years in a Communist prison had not broken that old man and he made it down to his knees, but not for long. Straight away the Pope hauls him up and then hugs him, really hugs him. There wasn't a dry eye in the house.

This was the eyewitness account of an extraordinary event in the autumn of 1996 when Pope John Paul was celebrating fifty years of priesthood and he invited any priest in the world who was celebrating also his golden jubilee to join him in Rome.

The 'old Jesuit' was Anton Luli who was born in a small village in Northern Albania in June 1910 on the feast of St Anthony of Padua. He felt the call of God from an early age and whenever he was able he joined the Jesuits in his own homeland. By this stage, the Second World War was well advanced and Anton managed to get through his studies without too much disruption. However, once the war was over it seemed as if his troubles and those of all believers were only beginning.

The Communists took over control of the country and for the next fifty years Albania descended into a Stalinist hell under the brutal dictatorship of Enver Hoxha. It was a regime that prided itself on being the world's only officially atheist state – no religion at all was tolerated. The Church and faith went underground, for churches were turned into cinemas and stores, museums and factories. Those who remained faithful had to celebrate their faith quietly, even away from the eyes and ears of their own children, for a child could so innocently betray a family by simply sharing something 'new that they had done last night' in the school playground. The secret police would be sure to call.

At the Mass in the Vatican on November 7 1996, various priests of the same year group as John Paul shared their testimony of what their years of priesthood had meant to them. Karol Wojtyla could certainly have equalled them all in terms of his own path to priesthood and his years of suffering in post-war Communist Poland. However, it was the words of Anton Luli that touched them all. It is best to let Anton share his own thoughts:

> I had recently become a priest when the Communist regime took over in my country, Albania, with its most ruthless religious persecution. Some of my confreres after a trail of lies and deceit were shot and died as martyrs of the faith. Like bread broken and blood poured out for my country's salvation, they celebrated their last personal Eucharist. It was 1946.
>
> Instead the Lord asked me to live. Opening my arms and letting myself be nailed to the cross, thus I celebrated my Eucharist, my priestly offering in the ministry denied me, with a life spent in chains and every kind of torture. On December 19 1947 they arrested me and charged me with propaganda against the government. I lived in solitary confinement for 17 years and for many more in forced labour. My first prison in

that freezing month of December was a lavatory in a village situated in the mountains of Shkodre. I stayed there for nine months, forced to crouch on hardened excrement and never being able to stretch out because the space was so small. On Christmas night that year (how could I forget?) they dragged me from that place and put me in another lavatory and then forced me to strip. A rope was passed under my arms. I was naked and could barely touch the ground with my toes. I felt my body slowly failing me. The cold gradually crept up my limbs and when it reached my chest and my heart was about to give in I gave a desperate cry. That night – in that place and in the solitude of that first torture – I experienced the real meaning of the incarnation and of the cross.

But in this suffering I had beside me and within me the comforting presence of the Lord Jesus. At times his support was something I can only call "extraordinary", so great was the joy and comfort he communicated to me. But also I have never felt resentment for those who robbed me, humanly speaking, of my life. After my release I met one of my torturers in the street and I was able to go up and embrace him. They released me in the amnesty of 1989. I was 79 years old.

This was my experience as a priest throughout these years. It was a very unusual experience compared to that of many priests, but certainly not unique. The priest is first and foremost someone who has known love; he is a man who lives in order to love – to love Christ and to love everyone in him to the point of giving up his life. Everything can be taken from us, but no one can wrench from our hearts our love for Jesus or our love for our brothers and sisters. Today, as in the past, we can say with conviction the words of St Paul: "who can separate us from the love of Christ? Shall tribulation or distress or persecution or famine or nakedness or the sword? No, in all these things we are more than conquerors through him who loved us." (Romans 8:35-7)

Holy Father, it is true; fifty years have passed since our ordination to the priesthood, but love for Jesus, love of Jesus never ages.

Fr Anton died two years later in 1998, a martyr to Christian faith.

JOHN MAIN

It must be twenty years ago now but that week was significant in my life. I have to confess I had never heard of Laurence Freeman, or John Main for that matter, but the Bishop asked me to 'look after' the former when he came to Belfast for a series of talks on prayer. I duly set up a series of meetings with people during the following week – lay faithful, religious, priests – introducing them, or should I say, facilitating them to be introduced to the spirituality of John Main – through the words and witness of Fr Laurence. In those days I too meditated and allowed the ancient but ever new method of Main to touch my soul.

John Main had such an interesting life. He had had a lot of experience – from soldier to lawyer and civil servant in the foreign Office in Malaysia. Even his father's posting with the Western Union Cable Company at Ballinskelligs in County Kerry may have had a mysterious influence on John's later life, being so close as it was to the ancient monastic settlements of Skellig Michael (6th–12th centuries).

In time all of these led him to enter a monastery himself. The year was 1959 as he entered the Benedictine abbey at Ealing in London and so began the next phase of his multifaceted life. But becoming a monk only opened the door on a different kind of spiritual search to find the contemporary relevance of monastic life in the modern world.

Main was increasingly struck by the great spiritual hunger that was afflicting the world. He felt there was a loss of the sacred at the heart of man, which could only be filled by prayer. He wanted to find a kind of prayer that was relevant to the modern world. Years before he had met a Hindu Swami who had contrasted – perhaps somewhat unfairly – the 'wordiness' of so much of Christian prayer – as he saw it – with the simplicity of the mantra – the repetition of a word or phrase – which was a common method in the East.

This led Main to rediscover something that had been at the heart of Christian prayer too – but many centuries before. John knew of the writings and methods of John Cassian, one of the so-called Desert Fathers. Cassian (360–435) had recommended such a discipline, the constant repetition of certain sacred words as a way of emptying the mind of ideas and rooting oneself in the divine mystery. Cassian had suggested the ancient Aramaic prayer *'maranatha'* (Come Lord Jesus) and Main also adopted this for his own personal use. Indeed what Main had learnt from the Hindu monk, Cassian had learnt from the Desert Fathers, and Benedict had learnt from Cassian. Main had rediscovered the Christian roots of this form of meditation.

Main wrote:

> you should choose a word that has been hallowed over the centuries by our Christian tradition. The word *"maranatha"* for instance means "Come Lord Jesus", a word Paul uses at the end of his first letter to the Corinthians. This prayer word is recited slowly, interiorly. The speed is fairly slow, fairly rhythmical. We begin by saying the mantra in our mind... then the mantra begins to sound not so much in our head but rather in our heart... then in the very depths of our being... and so meditation becomes a process of self discovery and integrating one's body, mind and spirit.

Fr Laurence in his time with us had also suggested using other words like 'Jesus' or 'Abba'.

There were other influences too. Main spent some time in Thomas Merton's monastery at Gethsemani in Kentucky. He wrote to a friend: 'my purpose in coming here was to talk to the community about prayer but in fact I have learnt so much myself while I have been here.' When John celebrated Mass in Merton's little chapel, he was able to say that 'I have just celebrated the most loving Mass of my life.' There is no doubt that when John stood in silence at the altar of Merton's hermitage, he understood the other pilgrim who had arrived with the Master.

In 1975 Main began a small prayer group at Ealing Abbey to experiment with this new – yet ancient – form of Christian prayer. Many lay people were attracted to Main's circle, confirming his belief that he had discovered a style of prayer that was accessible and useful for lay people too. Indeed it led him to consider the possibility of a new type of monasticism in which monks, nuns and lay people might be able to share a common life of prayer and work together.

In 1977 the opportunity came to put his vision into practice – the bishop, Leonard Crowley, of the city of Montreal in Canada, invited John to launch the experiment of which he was thinking. The Benedictine priory there became a centre that attracted people from all over the world. Main's writings also began to become known far beyond the priory and local prayer circles were formed around the world. Many were witnessing to the way in which their lives were being transformed by the simple practice of meditating for half an hour once or twice a day.

Sadly little time was given to Main to develop his experimental monastery. In 1982 he was discovered to be in an advanced state of lung cancer. His last months were spent in terrible pain and demanding treatments; yet he was uncomplaining and few, even of his friends, knew of his condition. He died in December surrounded by his Benedictine community and Montreal meditators. One of them summed up his life: '..if one were to characterise his life in one sentence it would be that he rediscovered and lived the simplicity of the Gospel' .

Leopold Mandic

Anyone who has ever visited the town of Medjugorje in Bosnia will no doubt have gone to Mass in the parish church of St James, whose twin spires dominate the town and the horizon. Of course, the jury is still 'out' on the alleged Marian apparitions there and the Church has still officially to pronounce its verdict. However, in the meantime, many hundreds of thousands are being blessed each year as they gather there to pray and seek peace in their lives.

Those who go to Mass in the parish church will also probably try to go to confession. For some it is part of the pilgrimage; for others it may be the first time in many a year as they seek to make a return to the faith of their youth. Everything is peaceful and calm as the penitents wait patiently for their turn to come. The confessionals to the left of the church carry the languages the priests are hearing in. But at the end of the row there is a statue of a Capuchin friar. Initially many on seeing it think it is a small imitation of the original priest but Leopold Mandic was actually this height in life – no more than four feet five inches.

Leopold was born on May 12 1866 in the town of Castelnuovo in Dalmatia (Croatia), the 12 child of very devout parents. He was baptised Adeodatus (literally 'given by God') and from an early age wanted to be a foreign missionary. In his heart and mind he said he was 'always beyond the seas.' In due time he entered the Capuchin order in response to a priestly vocation and was professed in 1885 and ordained priest in 1890 in Venice. After various assignments within the order he ended up in Padua in 1906.

Every human being has at least one secret ambition, one silent dream that breaks the daily tedium and teases the senses. Some may dream of being adventurers in far off lands; others of becoming film stars or winning some talent contest; others of discovering some lost star or unique scientific formula. And others God asks to give up their secret ambitions in order to serve Him and the Church. Leopold Mandic was such a man who had to surrender his own heart's desire in order to accomplish God's will in his life and with this obedience he brought numerous graces to the people who came into his presence.

A few years after his assignment to Padua the First World War broke out and Leopold found himself a prisoner, taken by the Austrians, and ministering in a camp as a priest to his fellow inmates. When he was eventually released, Leopold thought that then he might still fulfil that earlier missionary dream, but his superiors sent him to various houses where he worked as a confessor and spiritual director. His own personal holiness and his unique insight into the human soul led his superiors to take this decision. While his own desire had been to preach the word of God, sadly his speech was often slow and laboured, almost stuttering. And so a ministry in the pulpit was out of the question. The confessional was to become Leopold's vocation and his charism for the next four decades of his life. Indeed he repeatedly prayed 'One flock, one shepherd' and offered up his apostolate in the confessional for this wider intention.

Leopold was always frail and he suffered from severe stomach ailments and chronic arthritis. These conditions were not helped by the numerous hours he spent in the confessional. However, he did not complain. In time he walked with a pronounced stoop and arthritis crippled his hands severely. Despite this he kept up his gruelling schedule and offered up his pain and discomfort to Our Lady of Sorrows, to whom he had a special devotion, calling her 'Parona Benedeta' (my holy boss).

Leopold transformed his confessional into an experience of human dignity and a personal encounter with the compassionate Lord. There every penitent experienced the mercy of God and the kindness of one particular priest. He once remarked 'some say that I am too good. But if you come and kneel before me, isn't this a sufficient proof that you want to have God's pardon?' To those who accused him of too lenient penances he would respond 'if the Lord wants to accuse me of showing too much leniency towards sinners, I'll tell him that it was he who gave me this example, and I haven't even died for the salvation of souls as he did.' Often he would say to a troubled soul 'be at peace; place everything on my shoulders. I will take care of it.' At night he would spend long hours in prayer – 'I must do penance for my penitents.' Indeed, one of those penances was his own living quarters – an extremely small room which was an icebox in winter and an oven in summer.

Leopold died on July 30 in 1942, during the height of the Second World War. In addition to the hours daily spent in the confessional, he was a frequent visitor to the nursing homes and hospitals in the Padua area. He once said of priests: 'a priest must die from apostolic hard work; there is no other death worthy of a priest.' His funeral was attended by the many people whom he had helped during those long hours and years in the confessional. Leopold's example was deeply respected in Rome and Paul VI beatified him in 1976 while it fell to Pope John Paul II to canonise him on October 16 1983, declaring him the saintly hero of the confessional. 'His greatness lay… in immolating himself, in giving himself, day after day, for the entire span of his priestly life'. Leopold the confessor was 'truly a missionary in another sense.'

MARY MCKILLOP

Mary Helen was a bit of a rebel, but she never meant to be! A century has now passed since the death of Mary Helen McKillop and over a decade since her beatification, but she is the first native Australian saint. She was the foundress of a remarkable congregation, the Sisters of St Joseph, who devoted themselves to providing free education and other services to the poor at a time when a young nation was just finding its feet.

Mary might also serve as the patron saint of all who have suffered the persecution of narrow-minded religious authorities, convinced they are acting in the place of God. That Mary remained free of bitterness, despite her ordeals, is considerable evidence of her holiness and a just cause for her honour.

She was born in 1842, in the great city of Melbourne in Southern Australia. Her parents, as the name suggests, were poor Scottish immigrants. After schooling, Mary took up the idea of being a governess for a wealthy family. But it was while working there that she met a charismatic young priest called Julian Woods, who inspired her to consider a religious vocation. Together they had the idea of starting a congregation dedicated to the needs of the poor. In what was a relatively young nation, there were many who had come from Europe – and especially Ireland and Scotland – in hope of fortune and a new life, and found that the reality was very different. In response to this call, in 1866, Mary put on a simple black dress and the next year she took religious vows – it was the start, however humble, of a new congregation in the Church.

From the beginning, Mary wanted her new sisters to be a congregation suited to the needs and demands of the Australian scene. So there were no distinctions between 'lay' and 'choir' sisters; there was to be radical equality. Also the sisters adhered to a strict vow of poverty. Most important of all, however, was her insistence that the congregation be subject to a 'central government'. This meant that instead of allowing each of her far-flung communities to be administered under the authority of the local bishop, they would be governed by an elected mother general, who would answer directly to Rome. This provision proved to be a source of great tension between the congregation and the Australian bishops in the years ahead.

Yet in almost no time Mary had attracted scores of young women to her congregation and houses were established in a number of cities and outback posts. At a time when almost no public services were provided for the poor, the Sisters of St Joseph won the admiration and gratitude of Australians of all classes and religious persuasions. The sisters followed farmers, miners and railway workers to the isolated outback regions; wherever these men and their families had to go in search of work, the sisters went to provide for their material and spiritual needs. Initially many of the bishops were eager to welcome the sisters into their dioceses, but often they tried to interfere in the management and direction of the sisters' work. Mary resisted this stoutly.

Sadly this initial support gave way to harassment and vilification. In one dramatic episode, one local bishop actually excommunicated Mary. Though he later rescinded this order on his deathbed, Mary and the congregation continued to operate under a cloud. Another bishop expelled her from his diocese and refused the sisters any leave to raise funds. The Bishop of Queensland sent damning letters to Rome claiming that the sisters were 'infected with fanaticism and insubordination to authority'.

Mary was determined to defend her work and that of the sisters, and travelled to Rome spending two years there seeking authorisation for her constitutions. Eventually she had an audience with Pope Pius IX who was personally intrigued by the story of the nun who had been excommunicated. When she returned to Australia she held up a papal document, which formally approved her congregation. Still the persecution did not cease. A team of other clerics, claiming also to be authorised by Rome, subjected the Sisters to a rigorous 'visitation' – seizing financial records and interviewing the sisters to discover scurrilous information about Mother Mary. Later it was learnt that the visitation had no backing from the Holy See and Mother Mary was completely exonerated. Rome finally came to her rescue and allowed the congregation to remain under central government.

Although she suffered greatly from the constant attacks over the years on her virtue and her faith, Mary referred to such ordeals as 'presents from God'. Innocent suffering was an opportunity, she believed, to shoulder the cross and so to grow closer to God. She never became bitter against the Church leaders who had opposed her. Indeed this forgiving attitude was complemented by the outstanding work of the congregation. Protestants and Catholics loudly praised her charity to the poor and her own personal poverty. Nevertheless she did acknowledge that 'God's presents were often hard to understand'.

Mother Mary lived on to see her congregation firmly established throughout Australia and New Zealand. She herself passed away after many years of painful illness on August 5 1909. She was laid to rest at the Gore Hill cemetery, a few miles north of Sydney. After her burial, people continuously took earth from around her grave, and as a result her remains were exhumed and transferred to a vault in a newly built church in Mount Street, Sydney. In 1973 Mother Mary became the first Australian to be formally proposed to Rome as a candidate for sainthood and in due course she was beatified by Pope John Paul on November 27 1994.

JOSEPH MOSCATI

The doctors did not hold out much hope. 'Julie', my parishioner, was in intensive care and there were tubes and monitors everywhere. Her liver had nearly ceased to function, her kidneys had been damaged and there was no hope of a transplant. Her husband and family were distraught; heaven was being stormed. I attended her twice in the ICU and at one of my daily Masses I asked the primary school children in attendance to pray for 'someone', keeping in mind the method of St Francis Xavier who always invited children to pray for those who were sick in their villages. Invariably they were healed and Francis was then able to tell people about Jesus.

Last night 'Julie' rang me from hospital to thank me for all the prayers. She had recovered from the coma and was soon to be discharged. I was astounded to hear her and together we thanked God. Remembering the condition of this girl just a few days before I also recalled the words of Scripture, which lead me to the saint I now wish to honour: 'there are cases when good health depends on doctors. They too will pray to the Most High to grant relief and healing in order to save life.' (Sirach 38:13-14) Joseph Moscati lived these verses.

Joseph was born in July 1880 in Benevito, a small town near Naples in Italy. He was the seventh of nine children of Francis and Rosa, who were a devout Christian couple. Francis was a lawyer who eventually became a judge in the local courts. Despite the anti-clericalism of the time, Francis and Rosa endeavoured to rear their children in the knowledge and practice of their faith. Often on walks they would visit one of the many beautiful churches that surrounded the city of Naples. This practice had a deep effect on Joseph – so much so that he himself would never begin his day as a doctor without attending Mass and receiving Holy Communion.

After going through the local schools with distinction, Joseph found himself attracted to medicine. His home was close to the local hospital for those who were incurable. Daily the sight of the sick and the suffering drew him closer to the field of medicine, and it was in this faculty that he enrolled in the University of Naples. However, it was also caring for his older brother Alberto who as a soldier had sustained severe head trauma and needed constant care at home that drew Joseph to love and care for the sick all his life. By the age of twenty-two he had begun to practise as a doctor, having passed the degree with first class honours. He had imbibed a spirit which no books could give – 'Happy are we doctors who are so often unable to alleviate suffering; happy if we remember that, as well as the body, we have before us the immortal soul, concerning which it is essential to remember the gospel precept to love them as ourselves. The sick represent Christ for us.'

Throughout his life Joseph kept a spiritual diary, which recorded his thoughts and reflections. Dealing as he did every day with death, this enabled him to see beyond the temporal life that was on a bed before him. A moment in his childhood had contributed to this awareness. He was looking at the hospital from his home one day and was seized with the passing of all things, like the falling petals from the flowers of nearby orange trees. 'The grandeur of death is not the end, but the beginning of the Sublime and the Divine, in whose presence flowers and beauty are as nothing.'

There were moments of great heroism too in his life as a doctor.

The volcano at Mt Vesuvius near Naples had begun to erupt, and a thick cloud of ash was falling on an outlying hospital where there were many elderly and infirm patients. Joseph went himself to evacuate the staff and the patients and shortly after the last one had left the roof of the hospital collapsed. Heroism of another sort was required when Italy entered the First World War. He entered the medical corps and was appointed as director of the office for the assistance of soldiers who were wounded or ill. During the war, he treated more than 3,000 wounded soldiers. Joseph was always delighted to see them recover but even more delighted when many of them returned to the practice of their faith and began again to attend Mass and the sacraments.

Back in his hospital after the war, he often encouraged his patients, especially those about to undergo surgery, to receive the sacraments first. 'Remember,' he wrote to a colleague, 'that you must treat not only bodies but also souls, with counsel that appeals to their minds and hearts rather than with cold prescriptions to be sent in to the pharmacist.' Indeed such was his brilliance that he could easily have pursued an academic career as a professor in the university, but Joseph preferred to continue working with his patients and to train the young aspiring doctors. This devotion to the sick would take its toll.

One day in 1927, Joseph began his day in the usual way by going to Mass and receiving Holy Communion. Then he made his round of the hospital. But after a midday meal, he felt tired and lay down and simply passed away. He was not yet 47 years old. The miracles came quickly, and he was beatified by Pope Paul VI in 1975 and canonised by Pope John Paul II during the Synod on the laity in 1987. He was a most fitting example of the holiness of the layman in the world.

St Joseph Moscati, teach us how to pray and care for those who are sick.

FRANCIS XAVIER
NGUYEN VAN THUAN

The helicopters rose slowly from the embassy roof, their blades whipping up the dust in some sort of apocalyptic symbol for the chaos that was all around. Dozens had tried desperately to clamber onto the metal birds even as they rose but only a few were fortunate. Many others remained on the ground or in the embassy compound awaiting their fate for they knew the Vietcong were at the gates and there would be retribution for the years of resistance and perceived collaboration with the 'enemy'. The Americans were leaving, as the French before them − humbled by the steadfast resistance of a people over decades. Soon Vietnam would be Communist and Saigon would be renamed Ho Chi Minh City.

There were many who had been associated with the 'ancien regime', many who had made money from the American presence. There were many others − those with faith and those without, who did not believe that the Communist 'way' was the answer for their country. Many would be 're-educated' in the new prisons and work centres which would soon be established. One such was a bishop who had just been made coadjutor of the capital city before Vietnam fell to the Vietcong. Francis Xavier Nguyen Van Thuan had also been the nephew of Ngo Dinh Diem who had been the former president of the Republic of Vietnam. His faith and his suspected political connections made him doubly suspect in the eyes of the new rulers. In 1975 he was arrested and he spent the next thirteen years in prison as a political prisoner of the Communist regime. Nine of these years he spent in solitary confinement.

The story of Francis Xavier begins in 1928 in the parish of Phu Cam in the city of Hue in Vietnam. Politics and the Church were in his blood. He had learnt his faith at the knees of his devout mother. She taught him about the Vietnamese martyrs of earlier centuries, some of whom had been related to their own family. It was no surprise when he entered the minor seminary when he was young eventually receiving ordination on June 11 1953. Then there followed a period of further studies in Rome between 1955 and 1959 where he obtained a doctorate in canon law. He returned to his native Vietnam and ministered there firstly in hospital chaplaincy and then also as chaplain to a prison. It was to be a ministry prophetic of his own later fate. Soon his undoubted talents in the area of priestly formation were recognised and eventually he became rector of the seminary. Episcopal ordination would follow in 1967 and he served in a number of dioceses before coming as coadjutor to Saigon.

When the Americans left, Francis was arrested though never tried or sentenced, but spent the next thirteen years incarcerated. The years in prison were difficult, but Francis' faith sustained him. As often as he could, he celebrated Mass in secret with three drops of wine in the palm of his hand and the host smuggled inside a flashlight by his faithful co-diocesans on the outside. He in turn smuggled out his writings on the back of old calendars, which were then promoted and inspired his fellow countrymen and women and others beyond the shores of Vietnam.

He wrote:

> We made little containers from the paper of cigarette boxes
> to reserve the Blessed Sacrament. Jesus in the Eucharist was

always with me in my shirt pocket… they [the Catholics in the camp] all knew that Jesus was among them, that He is the One who cures all their physical and mental suffering. At night the prisoners would take turns keeping adoration; Jesus helped in a tremendous way with his silent presence. Many Christians regained the fervour of their faith during these days, and Buddhists and other non-Christians converted. The strength of the love of Jesus is irresistible. The darkness of prison became light, the seed germinated underground during the storm.

When eventually Francis was released in 1988, he was allowed by the government to visit his parents who were by this time in Australia. One can but imagine their reunion! His father passed away in 1993 and his mother lived on for several more years passing the milestone of 100 years! When in 1991 he was allowed to travel to Rome, he was not permitted to return to his native land but spent his remaining years in the Eternal City. Here his energy continued in his efforts for his beloved Vietnamese – in raising funds for a leprosarium, in the reconstruction of churches and in promoting the Vietnamese culture. He even was invited by Pope John Paul to preach the annual Lenten retreat to the Papal household in the Jubilee year 2000. The years of incarceration had also taken their toll, and Francis passed away in September 2002. His cause for beatification was begun in 2007.

One of the pieces of writing that Francis has left to the Church is his 'Ten Rules for a Catholic Life'. They are indeed the stuff of martyrs and the fabric of a saint:

1. I will live the present moment to the fullest.

2. I will discern between God and God's work.

3. I will hold firmly to one secret: prayer.

4. I will see in the Holy Eucharist my only power.

5. I will have only one wisdom: the science of the cross.

6. I will remain faithful to my mission in the Church and for the Church as a witness of Jesus Christ.

7. I will seek the peace the world cannot give.

8. I will carry out a revolution by renewal in the Holy Spirit.

9. I will speak one language and wear one uniform: charity.

10. I will have one very special love: the Blessed Virgin Mary.

FLANNERY O'CONNOR

The American writer, Flannery O'Connor, who was born in 1925, tells of an occasion when she was invited to a dinner party with a number of various literary 'glitterati' of the time. She was young and rather shy and was just beginning to make a name for herself in the literary world; so she contributed little to the conversation. Her host, Mary McCarthy, a writer too and a lapsed Catholic, tried to bring Flannery into the conversation. 'I think the Eucharist – as symbols go – is quite a good symbol, don't you think?' To her surprise Flannery found herself blurting out in response 'if it's just a symbol, then to hell with it!' It was one of those 'show-stopping' moments, but – now – everyone at the table was aware that she was there.

Flannery would have been embarrassed at the attention caused by her heartfelt comment. 'There won't be any biographies of me,' she once wrote,' because lives spent between the house and the chicken yard do not make exciting copy.' And yet her short life was significant in that at her death she had left behind a small output of stories and novels, which assured her place among the best of American writers. Born of the marriage to two of Georgia's oldest Catholic families in the 'Bible Belt', she herself was a devout believer who tried to convey in her writing the soul's struggle with the 'stinking mad shadow of Jesus.'

There was another significant factor too in her life – her health.

Her father had died from lupus and she too would in time succumb to this incurable and debilitating disease that sapped her energy and confined her to her mother's farm in the state of Georgia. There she wrote as her strength permitted – two hours in the morning – and later – as energy permitted – tended the menagerie of ducks and swans, peacocks and ostriches, with which she surrounded herself. She would not allow anyone to pity her plight, but her illness imposed on her a discipline, which she managed to turn to her art. 'I have enough energy to write and I can with one eye squinted take it all as a blessing.' Her faith enabled her to understand and accept her suffering and to turn it to a purpose.

Apart from her short stories, her weekly book reviews for the local diocesan paper and her few novels, she wrote many letters. Her friend Betty Hester, for instance, received a weekly letter for ten years. 'I write the way I do *because* I am a Catholic. However I am a Catholic peculiarly possessed of the modern consciousness... to possess this within the Church is to bear a burden...' For O'Connor the Catholic doctrines of creation, fall and redemption were the lens through which she viewed the world. In some ways her stories and characters reflected something of the writing of Thomas Hardy of a recent earlier era, but without the fatalism. For her there was an awareness that grace was mediated through nature. To her secular friends who were often amazed by her beliefs, she would reply that dogma was a source of liberation, for 'it preserves mystery for the human mind.'

Was Flannery's era any different from our own, when so many may be attracted by the figure of Christ but reject the Church? She believed that the Church was the only thing likely to make the world endurable. She could believe this and yet still acknowledge the Church's sins – indeed they were all the more painful for her. 'The only thing that makes the Church endurable is that it is somehow the Body of Christ and that on this we are fed.'

She had grown up during the thirties when Hitler and Nazism were coming to the fore. She was a young adult when Communism was spreading throughout postwar Europe and beyond. In America there was the Depression and a sense of hopelessness for so many. It was a 'religionless age', she wrote, 'when it was so much easier not to believe, when 'nihilism is the gas we breathe.' Elsewhere she wrote 'I think there is no suffering greater than what is caused by the doubts of those who want to believe. I know what torment this is. What people don't realise is how much religion costs. They think faith is a big electric blanket, when of course it is the cross.'

The characters that spill out of O'Connor's stories are a strange assortment of backwood fanatics and secular intellectuals, as well as ordinary country folk. Even some of their names suggest ironic clues as to their deficiencies – Tom Shiflet, Mary Grace, Hulga Hopewell, Mrs Cope. Often they are fundamentalist Protestants who undergo transformations of character that to O'Connor's thinking brought them closer to the Catholic mind. Her stories are set in that ground over which God and the Devil fight. Characters are pruned and emptied of their illusions and even sometimes their 'virtues' before they can face the truth. 'All my stories are about the action of grace on a character who is not very willing to support it.' 'Grace changes us and change is painful.' Ultimately she believed her stories were hopeful, in the same sense that she believed that purgatory was the most hopeful doctrine of the Church.

Flannery died from lupus on August 3 1964 – she was just thirty-nine years of age. In her last year she was able to finish a number of her short stories and she would have been quite happy to be remembered solely for these. However in death she has also achieved a reputation as a Christian apologist, making the life of faith seem reasonable and attractive even in the midst of doubts and questions.

FREDERIC OZANAM

It began with a few sticks on a cold winter night, but first let me digress a little to March 13 2013 – and Rome. 'At the Papal election Cardinal Claudio Hummes, archbishop Emeritus of Sao Paolo in Brazil, sat next to me' – a dear, dear friend, Jorge Bergoglio, related – 'When the votes reached two thirds, there was the usual applause because the Pope had been elected. He hugged me and said "do not forget the poor"' The cardinals knew Jorge's reputation – his simple lifestyle, travelling on the local bus, cooking his own meals, living in a simple apartment – all preparing him for the task of being 'Peter' in the modern Church. Francis was chosen.

Two hundred years ago this month, there was born a man who also would 'not forget the poor'. Frederic Ozanam, now Blessed, went on to found the great St Vincent de Paul Society, which has members in every continent and which is loved and respected by people of all walks of life – people who believe and those who don't.

Frederic loved his faith and was glad he had been born into it. His intelligence gave him a freedom and confidence to be able to defend it when necessary. Indeed Frederic was a man of great genius, obtaining first a doctorate on the subject of the great Italian poet, Dante, and then later completing his studies in law and obtaining the chair of commercial law in the University of Lyons.

When he came as a young man to the great university of the Sorbonne in Paris, he and some friends tried to get a debate going in order to present an intellectual witness to the faith. But one student heckled him at one of these sessions: 'You Christians are fine at arguing, but what do you do? What is your Church doing now? What is she doing for the poor of Paris? Show us your works and we will believe in you.' Frederic was stung by these words. At that moment one of his friends, Auguste, suggested some effort on behalf of the poor. Frederic realised that Christianity is not about words, but about deeds inspired by love. That night, he and one of his friends went out to collect firewood for a poor widow, and that was the beginning of the Society that we all know today.

In those early years of the Industrial Revolution, the poor who manned the factories lived in incredible squalor. It was the same right across Europe, especially in the cities, which were beginning to build factories, which in turn attracted the poor from the countryside in search of work. They were the people whom Victor Hugo immortalised in his great novel *Les Miserables*, which, of course, has been made into a musical and a recent film. They were extremely poor and they lived in diseased and overcrowded slums. Many children never saw their second birthday.

That small gathering of friends started as the 'Conference of History', but became very quickly the 'Conference of St Vincent de Paul'. They met for the first time in May 1833, and determined to engage in practical works of charity. It was to grow rapidly, and even during Frederic's lifetime it was to become well known not just in France, but throughout the world.

For Ozanam and his friends, their journey was literally 'crossing the tracks' into an unknown world, which even most of the clergy of the time did not know. The bourgeois intellectuals, who were so intoxicated with the slogans of the Revolution, were strangers to the world of the poor. Ozanam had at the beginning no programme of social reform, but his response was simply Christian charity and to enter literally into the areas where the poor lived. For Frederic, it was also a two way process – the poor are 'messengers of God to test our justice and our charity, and to save us by our works.'

There was also an apologetic side to the life and faith of Frederic. Having earned his doctorates, he lectured at the Sorbonne on the Catholic interpretation of history. He wanted to reconcile the teaching of the Church with the best features of the modern age. With other Catholics, he believed the Church must overcome its attitude of defensive isolation and nostalgia for a bygone age. The Church had nothing to fear from living in the present or looking to the future.

The revolution of 1848 brought about the explosion that Frederic and others feared. The workers threw up barricades – so immortalised in Hugo's novel – and turned Paris into a battle zone. The uprising was suppressed at a terrible cost. For many Catholics, the events confirmed their conservatism and their commitment to 'law and order'. Though Frederic deplored the violence that had ensued, he defended the justice of the workers' cause and continued to speak and act on behalf of those who were poor and voiceless.

All of this took its toll and Frederic's health broke down, leading him eventually to resign from his university work and public activity. He was a mere forty years old when he died. Yet seeds had been planted and fruit was already being borne, as the Society he had founded continued to grow and flourish. Even the French government, so often anticlerical since the revolution of 1789, invited the Society to help it in its work for alleviating the plight of the poor.

Frederic was beatified by Pope John Paul on August 22 1997, during the World Youth Day celebrations, which took place in Paris at that time. He was indeed a fitting model for the youth of every age and place. A society that began with a few sticks being collected is now known all over the world by the simple wooden box, which invites our response outside the church after Mass. 'Do not forget the poor'!

ELVIRA PETROZZI

I watched the elderly nun march purposefully across the yard. Coming towards her was a young man who was tall and well built. He was wearing work clothes and he was covered in dust. Yet when they met he gave her a great bear hug like some long lost friend. 'Isn't that Sr Elvira?' I said to a young man nearby. 'Isn't she the foundress?' 'Yes, it is; she is our mother; she is number one!' he replied.

To visit a Cenacle (Cenacolo in Italian) is a beautiful experience. It is to enter into another world where the hardness of the world is left behind and dreams are allowed to be fashioned. The Cenacolo community was founded by Sr Elvira Petrozzi, an Italian nun, in 1983. For many years she had been concerned by the destruction she had seen among young people through drug abuse and she longed to help them. Since she had no formal training to work with addicts, and the charism of her order was teaching, it was eight years before she managed to persuade her superiors that this was a genuine call from God and to release her for this work.

Elvira began with two companions, a fellow religious Sr Aurelia and a lay teacher Nives Grato. They begged for and obtained an old abandoned house in the city of Saluzzo in Italy. She had to pay the sum of one dollar a year to the local council, but on July 16, the feast of Our Lady of Mount Carmel, the Cenacle community was born. Sr Elvira said that a priest who had come to stay with them suggested this name and she liked it. She thought of the upper room where the disciples went out of fear after the crucifixion of Jesus. So many young people were full of fear, with so much loneliness and restlessness in their hearts.

Soon young people began arriving having heard of someone who wanted to help them in their desperation. Elvira began to care for them but it was a steep learning curve! In the beginning, the young drug addicts were allowed to smoke and even have a glass of wine – as Italians do – with their meal. But one night she returned to the house to find that all the young men in the community were drunk, having bored a hole in the kitchen wall in order to finish off the supplies of wine! So alcohol – and in time tobacco – were banned from the communities – and it was the young who made these decisions.

While secular detox programmes will use drug substitutes to wean people off drugs, Sr Elvira had a different approach. Many of these young people have tried to cope with their problems by turning to drugs. Their often selfish focus was simply the next 'fix'. She wanted to show them that there was a much better way and that was Christ. Thus the Cenacle community was not so much a drug rehab centre as a school of life with prayer at its heart. To many it seemed initially like a spiritual 'boot camp' where they learned to live in a totally new way – to accept a simple lifestyle and to rediscover the gifts of work and friendship and faith in the Word of God, instead of relying on the crutch of drugs to escape from everything that was too painful. Through the work of the Cenacle the addict learned to embrace the suffering and pain in their lives and give it to Jesus in prayer and especially before the Blessed Sacrament.

One of the most important aspects of the Cenacle, which Elvira developed, was the role of the 'guardian angels', who were fellow addicts but further along the spiritual journey. They offered emotional and spiritual support to the young addict who may have just entered a community and was struggling. The 'angels' provide 24/7 support in terms of listening, encouraging, even making cups of tea for their young charges during the night. This unconditional love melts the hardest hearts and helps prepare the newcomer for the day when he or she too will be able to do the same for others.

In time many return to normal society and get jobs and eventually a spouse and family. But others remain on in the Cenacles to help others who have arrived at that same point where they were perhaps just a year or two before. Many married couples have been formed out of friendships forged in the Cenacle, though the boys and girls have separate communities. And – beautifully – a new religious order has grown up within the community from former addicts.

Today there are over 66 Cenacles throughout the world with the majority in Italy and the number is still growing. There is a Cenacle now in Ireland at Knock, opened on the feast of the Immaculate Conception in 1999. For Sr Elvira, her dream has come true and she is living to see it bear so much fruit around the world.

In October 2005, Pope Benedict honoured her by inviting her presence as an auditor at the Synod of the Eucharist. Her own deep faith in the Eucharist is perhaps the greatest reason for the success of the Cenacles. She shared with the Synod Fathers, 'The Eucharist is nourishment, much more filling than pasta or food for the body. The Eucharist is reconciliation, encounter, amazement, beauty, strength, risk. It gives you everything that you need to live each day, and it makes you learn so many things.' With such faith in the Eucharist, the Cenacle has become a place of healing and new dreams are made possible.

PATRICK PEYTON

Imagine Brad Pitt, Angelina Jolie, George Clooney and Meryl Streep, all lining up to talk on prime time television about the importance of prayer in their lives!

Hard to imagine? Yes, perhaps we do live in a different age! Yet fifty years ago the stars of Hollywood did just that. Only then it was Gary Cooper, Loretta Young, Lucille Ball, Henry Fonda and Jack Benny. Older readers will recall these names with a certain nostalgia!

The person who persuaded these megastars of the silver screen was not a bigshot impresario or a Mel Gibson shooting a new religious movie, but a priest whose humble beginnings were a far cry from the mansions of Hollywood and Beverley Hills. Patrick Peyton was born in 1909 in the parish of Attymass in County Mayo in Ireland. He was a member of a family of nine and life was tough. In those decades after the great potato famine of the 1840s, the economic situation in Ireland was very difficult indeed and many generations of families made their way to the boats, which took them to England, Australia and of course, the United States. Such was the path for Patrick and his brother Tom. Nellie, their sister, was already there and the brothers went to join her.

Patrick well remembered the moment of departure for him and his brother Tom. A day or so before they left, the father asked him to kneel before a picture of the Sacred Heart. 'He addressed Our Lord with an intensity from his heart as he entrusted me completely to His care and protection. Then he said words which were engraved on my heart: "Be faithful to Our Lord in America."'

Patrick's wish from boyhood was to be a priest and once he reached the States he was able to fulfil his dream. He enrolled in the seminary and made good progress. However in his final year he developed tuberculosis, which was a common ailment throughout the world – and in particular among the poor – in the first half of the 20th century. The illness devastated him and the medical team gave Patrick little hope of recovery, or at least full recovery. They didn't reckon on the power of prayer and the faith of this particular Irishman! He prayed especially to Our Lady and soon his health improved much to the consternation of the doctors. In 1941, Patrick was ordained with his brother Tom to the priesthood at the Basilica of the Sacred Heart on the campus of Notre Dame University.

He was so grateful to Our Lady that he asked his superiors if he could begin the Prayer Crusade, which was to take him all over the world preaching the importance of prayer and especially family prayer. He knew this lesson not from books and learned teachers, but on his knees and beside his parents and siblings:

> What impressed me most was the voice of my mother talking to Mary: "Holy Mary, Mother of God, pray for us sinners now and at the hour of our death." In good times and in bad, in sickness and health, in poverty and hard work, we ended each day speaking to Jesus and His Mother, offering them the greatest tribute that could possibly be given, making the greatest act of faith, and honouring Mary above all the angels and saints. Because of the daily family rosary my home was for me a crusade, a school, a university, a library and most of all a little church.

Like many great ventures for God, Patrick's Prayer Crusade had small beginnings. He had started a 15 minute programme on one of the local radio stations based on the simple idea of families saying the rosary together. It was shortly after his own ordination and America – like most of the rest of the free world – was at war. With so many men away fighting, families were suffering, indeed disintegrating. Patrick spoke to one of the radio chiefs at one of the larger companies and they agreed to give him a longer slot if he could persuade a big star to participate. He persuaded the parents of the Sullivan brothers to come on one of his first shows – their five boys had died together on a battleship in the Pacific. Then he went directly to Hollywood and asked to speak to Bing Crosby. To his surprise he was put through and the singing star and actor agreed also to participate.

Within a few years, Fr Peyton had a regular show called 'Family Theatre' running weekly on national radio. James Stewart who starred in many Hollywood films hosted the first one with these words: 'with the hope that families everywhere will always be together and that your home will be a happy one – with the conviction that prayer, simple prayer, will help keep it that way.'

'Family Theatre' had a basic message and always began with the words of Alfred Lord Tennyson 'more things are wrought by prayer than this world dreams of.' And, of course, before the end of the programme the famous slogan that became Fr Peyton's signature was also aired: 'the family that prays together stays together.' In time as the new era of television dawned, he embraced the new medium with enthusiasm and undertook the monumental task of producing 15 biblical dramas based on the mysteries of the rosary. In all, Family Theatre produced more than 58 films in Patrick's own lifetime, enlisting the talent of Hollywood's finest – from Frank Sinatra to William Shatner and Bing Crosby to Grace Kelly – indeed the last three films Princess Grace made before her marriage were for Family Theatre.

Patrick Peyton died in 1992 at the age of 83, but others had already taken up the baton of religious broadcasting, which he had started. His cause for canonisation was introduced in 2001 and today he bears the title 'Servant of God'.

JERZY POPIEŁUSZKO

Secular Commentators on the Solidarity period of Poland's recent history tend to interpret the life and death of Fr Jerzy Popiełuszko in political terms, that Fr Jerzy died at the hands of a tyrannical regime, and that he was not a martyr in the traditional Catholic sense. The Church took a very different view in beatifying the priest in June 2010.

The end of the Communist regime in Eastern Europe began with the election of Karol Wojtyla in 1978 to the throne of Peter. He was the first non-Italian Pope since Hadrian VI in the early sixteenth century. Within a few months, the new Pope visited his own homeland. The Communist regime was still strongly in power, but John Paul did not preach revolution against the authorities. He simply reminded his own people of their dignity as persons in Christ. 'Do not be afraid to insist on your rights. Refuse a life based on lies and double thinking. Do not be afraid to suffer with Christ.' It was the beginning of the end. Within a year of his visit, the militant trade union movement of Solidarity was born although it would be several years – and a period of martial law – before the Polish nation and Eastern Europe would be completely free.

Jerzy was born in the village of Okopy in Eastern Poland in 1947 and after secondary school entered the seminary in Warsaw. His training was interrupted for two years of military service, and during this time he was beaten several times for professing his Christian faith.

After ordination he held several appointments before being assigned to the parish of St Stanislaus Kostka in the city of Warsaw. He worked also with some health care personnel, and so was asked to organise the medical teams during the Pope's visits in 1979 and in 1983. August 1980 had seen the birth of the Solidarity movement and workers from the local steel plant requested someone to say Mass for them. The lot fell to Jerzy and he stayed with the workers night and day in their strike in support of their comrades in Gdansk. The lessons Jerzy learnt from the life of Maximilian Kolbe – spiritual freedom in the midst of physical enslavement – came to the fore. It was a struggle to affirm the spiritual nature of the human person and to reject a culture built on lies and fear.

The attitude of the regime hardened and Solidarity was banned in December 1981 and many leaders were imprisoned. Many lost their jobs and so the ability to support their families. Jerzy attended the trials of many of these activists, sitting prominently in court so that they could see they were not forgotten. His house became a centre for gathering food and clothes for the families whose breadwinner was behind bars. But it was in the court that he conceived the idea of a 'Mass for the Country', to be celebrated for the imprisoned and their families.

And so it began. It was not a political demonstration and Jerzy was adamant that there would be no banners or slogans. But the Masses became well known not just in Warsaw but throughout Poland and as many as 20,000 people were often in attendance. He insisted that change would be brought about slowly and peacefully and the sign of peace at the Mass was one of the most poignant moments imaginable in the context of the national struggle. He himself was not a powerful speaker but simply someone of deep conviction. 'To serve God is to seek a way to human hearts. To serve God is to speak about evil as a sickness, which should be brought to light so that it can be cured. To serve God is to condemn evil in all its manifestations.' He believed the Eucharist was truly the sacrament of non-violence – 'the way of Jesus to conquer evil and violence must be the Christian way: the way of non-violence, of love and forgiveness.'

Inevitably the authorities took notice. Jerzy could often tell which of the congregation were there to listen and pray and those who were there to inform on him and report back to the Communist bosses. They saw him as an enemy because he was freeing people from fear of the system. He was subjected to countless forms of petty harassment. He was followed wherever he went; sometimes his Masses were interrupted by hecklers. Most ominously, a bomb was hurled at his apartment. Jerzy was not deterred – 'the only thing we should fear is the betrayal of Christ for a few silver pieces of meaningless peace.'

Eventually they could take no more and in October 1984 the young priest was kidnapped by security agents on his way back to Warsaw from visiting a parish in a nearby town. He was savagely beaten and then his body was weighted down and thrown into a deep reservoir. His driver on the night had managed to escape and reported everything to the press. Some days later his body was discovered and there was a national outrage. Some commentators would suggest that this was one of the key events in hastening the complete demise of Communism in Poland. His funeral was a massive demonstration with over 250,000 people in attendance. In defiance of the law, many official delegations of Solidarity gathered to pay their respects. He was buried in the church cemetery where he had ministered and it is estimated that over 17 million people have visited his grave since, including Pope John Paul, in one of his later visits to his native land.

Fr Jerzy was beatified on June 6 2010, the feast of Corpus Christi, in Warsaw's Pilsudski square. His mother, Marianna, who had reached 100 years a few days earlier was present at the event.

Miguel Pro

'*Viva Cristo Rey!*' 'Long live Christ the King!' They were the last words shouted out by one of Mexico's bravest sons in the autumn of 1927.

When Pope John Paul visited the great country of Mexico in 1988 he was greeted at the Masses and on the cavalcades by millions of ecstatic men and women. It was a far cry from the earlier years of the century when persecution was the order of the day and the faith – if it was to survive at all – had to keep a low key and even go underground. In many ways the situation was not unlike Ireland during the Penal days of the 16 and 17 centuries.

Miguel Pro was born in January 1891 and grew up in a religious family. Two of his sisters entered the religious life and from an early age Miguel was attracted to do something special with his own life. At the age of 20 he entered the Jesuit order so that he could devote his life to the service of God. However within a couple of years he had to flee the country along with many of his fellow Jesuits. First he went to Spain and then to Belgium to continue his studies and be ordained a priest on August 31 1925. Sadly his family were unable to be with him at the ceremony but he felt spiritually present to each of them and afterwards he took out their photos and individually blessed them.

His first assignment was to work with the miners of Charleroi in Belgium. Despite the Communist tendencies of many of the workforce he was able to reach them through his own joy and gentle spirit. All of this despite the fact that he had to undergo a series of operations for some stomach ulcers he had incurred.

In the summer of 1926 his superiors sent Pro back to Mexico in the hope that a change of climate would help his health. However, the political situation was if anything worse than when he had left. Plutarco Calles was now President of Mexico. Unlike his predecessors he vigorously enforced the anti-Catholic provisions of the 1917 constitution, especially the so called 'Calles law', which provided specific penalties for priests who criticised the government or who wore clerical garb outside their churches. Some Mexican states even closed churches and actively pursued a policy of hunting down and killing any priest they might find. The powerful novel *The Power and the Glory* by the English Catholic novelist Graham Greene is based on this era in Mexican history.

Pro, like many of his confreres, had to go 'underground' and celebrate the Eucharist and the other sacraments whenever and wherever he could. He himself left a legacy of letters describing his ministry during 1926–7 and always he signed with a nickname 'Cocol', a colloquial name given to a local sweet bread, which Miguel especially liked when he was a child. In particular he worked with the poor of the capital, Mexico City, and often provided for their temporal needs as well as their spiritual.

Often too he had to adopt many disguises in order to carry out his mission. He became known throughout the city as the 'underground priest' – much to the annoyance of the authorities. Often he would show up in the middle of the night dressed as a beggar or a street sweeper to baptise children or hear confessions. Several times he slipped into the police station disguised as an officer in order to give the last rites to those destined for execution in the morning. Once he escaped the police by a matter of seconds, only to return a few minutes later in the guise of a police inspector and demanded to know of a junior officer why they hadn't caught 'that rascal Pro'! On another occasion, he slipped out of a taxi, which was being pursued by police cars, lit a cigar and began strolling arm in arm with a very attractive and surprised young lady. The police sped past, paying no attention to the romantic couple on the pavement!

An abortive assassination attempt was made on the former President of the country, Alvaro Obregon. The state had a pretext to arrest Pro, this time along with his brothers. Despite the fact that one of the ringleaders confessed his part in the plot and that the Pro brothers had nothing to do with it, President Calles gave orders for Miguel to be executed. He even had the execution meticulously photographed in the hope that the event would deter any other rebels from defying the government. On the morning of November 29 1927, Miguel walked from his cell and as he passed the firing squad he blessed the soldiers. He was allowed to bring with him a crucifix and a rosary. About the latter he had once stated 'here is my weapon. With it along I have no fear of anyone.' Then just before they raised their rifles to fire he spread his arms and cried out '*Viva Cristo Rey!*' When the shots of the firing squad failed to kill him an officer shot him at point blank range.

When Miguel was buried, thousands defied the authorities by making a public display of mourning. Vast crowds walked behind the cortege and more than 500 cars formed the procession to his final resting place. At the funeral an elderly woman had her sight miraculously restored.

Pope John Paul beatified Miguel on September 18 1988 and spoke these words: 'he is a new glory for the beloved Mexican nation as well as for the Society of Jesus. Indeed the deepest root of self-sacrificing surrender for the lowly was his passionate love for Jesus Christ and his ardent desire to be conformed to him, even unto death.'

EDEL QUINN

'The glory of God is in a fully alive person,' the great bishop and saint of Lyon, Irenaeus, wrote in the second century. Another saint of a different era, Teresa of Avila, remarked on one occasion, 'From long-faced saints deliver us, O Lord'.

The person I want to talk to you about is not yet a canonised saint of the Church, but she is in the waiting room. She certainly qualifies as a person who lived life to the full, and was far from the long-faced saints feared by St Teresa.

Edel Quinn was born in Kanturk in County Cork in 1907. Her father and mother were devout parents, but because of her father's job as a bank clerk, the family were often on the move, and the young Edel found herself attending schools in Clonmel and Cahir, Enniscorthy and Tralee.

From early on, daily Mass was very much part of her routine, but she combined devotion with a great zest for life. She learned to play the piano and violin, and enjoyed swimming and tennis. She even learned the movements of Spanish dancing, and taught these to an appreciative local following.

Following school, Edel began work as a typist. Her first employer would eventually sell-up shop and enter the Beda seminary for older vocations in Rome. In due time, Mr O'Hanlon became a priest. Her new employer was French. Pierre was enchanted by Edel's good looks and her warm personality. Often the two would play tennis and even dance and party together. In a short time Pierre realised he was in love with this beautiful woman but, sadly for him, his love was not reciprocated.

Edel confided one evening that she wanted to become a contemplative nun. Pierre was shattered, but would remain always grateful to Edel for the many happy memories she had left him.

Before her plans to enter the convent were realised, however, there was another chapter in her life, which ultimately would prove to be decisive. It was while she was working in Dublin that she first came into contact with the Legion of Mary, a lay organisation, which had just begun life in that city. It became famous for its street ministry and door-to-door outreach, as well as other spiritual works of mercy.

Soon, Edel's dedication and efficiency were noted, and she was appointed to lead a branch of the Legion, called a Praesidium. It ministered to women in one of the poorest areas of inner-city Dublin. Many of these women fell into prostitution to make ends meet. Often, Edel would visit these women after a long day in the office as a typist.

Edel's reading of the writings of St Therese of Lisieux made a deep impression on her, as she tried to emulate the Little Flower's practice of doing little things as perfectly as possible. She would often endeavour to find opportunities to make small and hidden sacrifices. Edel would spend at least half an hour before the Blessed Sacrament each day, and she would also recite all fifteen of the Mysteries of the Rosary.

Her health intervened, however, when she was diagnosed as having a severe case of tuberculosis, and had to spend a period of eighteen months in a sanatorium. On her recovery, she resumed her work as a typist and some of her Legion duties, even to the point of volunteering to go to England to help bolster the faith there.

Then there came a call from the bishops of Zanzibar and Nairobi for a Legion envoy to go out to start groups of lay people to evangelise Africa. As soon as she heard the call, this sickly young woman knew that that was where God wanted her, and that he would provide the strength. Needless to say, there was plenty of opposition from family and friends, and even from Legion members, who thought someone stronger should go.

However, the Legion council obviously heard the Lord's voice, and Edel was duly sent. For the next few years, Edel went from mission station to mission station, through difficult territory, in ten vast dioceses of East Africa, forming lay leaders to evangelise their own people. It was peer evangelisation, and it was rooted in the culture of the area.

Edel would never let her own standards slip. Despite the problems of the terrain and sometimes of the transport, she always insisted that people turn up for meetings, and she herself set the standard in this regard. The sound of her old car often pierced the silence of the African night, but was also a welcome sound in the mission stations.

The earlier years of ill-health in Ireland began to take their toll, however. One visit to Malawi in 1941 was particularly perilous. She arrived at a convent one night, and was immediately put to bed by the French Canadian sisters, one of whom stayed with her all night. In the morning, Edel whispered: 'Don't worry about me, Sister. Our Lady has told me that I have three more years to work for her'. Finally her health did give out, in 1944, and she died and was buried in Nairobi.

Often, when people quote those lines of St Irenaeus about a person being fully alive, they omit the second half of the sentence: 'and that person is fully alive who sees God face to face'. Edel, who lived life to the full, was now more alive than ever.

On December 15 1994, Pope John Paul declared Edel Venerable, and the beatification process is proceeding satisfactorily.

A simple poem by her close friend and fellow Legionary, Mona

Tierney, was one of Edel's favourites. It is a fitting way to end:

> *What is all, when all is told,*
> *That ceaseless striving for fame and gold,*
> *The passing joys and the bitter tears?*
> *We are only here for a few short years.*
> *What is all, just passing through?*
> *A cross for me and a cross for you.*
> *Ours seemed heavy when others' seemed light,*
> *But God in the end sets all things right.*
> *He tempers the dark with heavenly gold,*
> *And that is all when all is told.*

OSCAR ROMERO

We watched their tears and felt their pain, albeit at a distance. The occasional television news item and the excellent coverage by our local Catholic press and missionary magazines fed our Irish interest and concern. Their troubles somehow mirrored our troubles, though their numbers of dead and injured were tenfold ours. El Salvador struck a chord in the hearts and minds of many Irish.

Thankfully, all that is a long time ago. The nation and its people have emerged from their internecine strife. With difficulty they are emerging into a better future, though not without growing pains. As anniversaries appear on the horizon, it is good to remember now the heroes who helped to form the way for peace and who ultimately paid the price for their courage. It was the Chilean dictator Pinochet, who coined the words 'we have nothing against ideas. We're against people spreading them.' Oscar Arnulfo Romero was both a man of ideas and a man intent on spreading them.

The selection of Oscar Romero as archbishop of San Salvador delighted the ruling powers of the country as much as it disappointed the activist clergy of the diocese. Known as a pious and relatively conservative bishop, there was nothing in his background to suggest he would challenge the status quo. He was born in 1917 in the mountain region of El Salvador and left school at 12 to begin an apprenticeship as a carpenter. He had shown promise as a craftsman, but while still very young had gone to seminary. After ordination in 1944, he had a period in a parish before becoming, for 23 years, the secretary to the country's bishops. He himself was to be ordained bishop in 1970 as auxiliary to the archbishop of El Salvador and he succeeded him four years later.

No one foresaw that he would become the 'voice of the voiceless', or as one theologian called him, 'a gospel for El Salvador'. Soon he would earn the hatred of the rich and powerful and also the disdain of some of his fellow bishops and he would become the first bishop to be slain at the altar since Thomas Becket in the 12th century.

Something changed him. Within weeks of his consecration he found himself officiating at the funeral of his friend, Rutilio Grande, a Jesuit who had been assassinated as a result of his commitment to social justice. Romero was deeply shaken by this event which marked a new level of violence in the country. Some spoke of a conversion in Romero. From being a somewhat timid and rather conventional cleric, he became an outspoken champion of justice. His monthly pastoral letters and weekly sermons, which were broadcast on the national radio, became a feature of life in the nation of El Salvador. He became the conscience of the nation and people listened avidly to his words.

The anomaly in the Salvadorian situation was that the persecutors called themselves Christians and often saw their cause as a crusade against Communism and subversion. One poster bore the legend 'Be a patriot! Kill a priest!' Romero saw the Church's option for the poor as a defining characteristic of Christian faith. 'A church that does not unite itself to the poor in order to denounce the injustice committed against them is not truly the Church of Jesus Christ,' he wrote. On another occasion, he said these unequivocal words: 'We either serve the life of Salvadorans or we are accomplices in their death... we either believe in a God of life or we serve the idols of death.'

During these final years and months in which Romero spoke, the nation was slipping rapidly towards anarchy. Coups, counter coups and fraudulent elections were the order of the day. The death squads roamed mercilessly at night suppressing the popular demand for justice. On March 23 1980, the day before his death, Romero appealed directly to members of the military: 'we are your people; the peasants you kill are your own brothers and sisters. In the name of God, in the name of our tormented people whose cries rise up to heaven, I beseech you, I beg you, I command you, stop the repression.'

The next day, as he was saying Mass in the chapel of the Carmelite sisters' cancer hospital where he lived, a single rifle shot rang out and struck Romero in the heart while he was raising up the bread and wine at the offertory – he died instantly. A few minutes before in his sermon he had said 'those who surrender to the service of the poor through love of Christ will live like the grain of wheat that dies.'
Even during his funeral, which was attended by a huge number of people including some Irish bishops, there was violence orchestrated by the regime. However, to the people of El Salvador, Romero was a martyr and a saint. He himself foresaw that he might well die a violent death. Two weeks before he had said these prophetic words:

I have frequently been threatened with death. I must say that, as a Christian, I do not believe in death but in the resurrection. If they kill me I shall rise again in the Salvadoran people. Martyrdom is a great gift from God that I do not believe I have earned. But if God accepts the sacrifice of my life, then may my blood be the seed of liberty, and a sign of hope that will soon become a reality... a bishop will die, but the Church of God – the people – will never die.

The thirtieth anniversary of Romero's death has come and gone. May our hearts continue to raise up in prayer all those who preach the Gospel 'welcome or unwelcome' and all who suffer for the poor of Christ.

STANLEY ROTHER

'To shake the hand of an Indian is a political act.' Those were the words of an ordinary Oklahoma farm boy, who never imagined that he would pose a threat to anyone who was rich and powerful. Yet in the early hours of July 28 1981, Fr Stanley Rother was murdered in the rectory of the church of Santiago Atitlan, where he had been serving in the land of Guatemala in Central America for thirteen years.

Thoughts of death were certainly far from Stanley's mind when he volunteered some years before in 1968. In the period after the second Vatican Council, there had been a great opening of hearts and minds in many of the Churches of the 'First World'. There was a genuine desire to identify with the poor, and many dioceses in Europe and the United States began to 'twin' with their counterparts in the so-called 'Third World'. Stan's home diocese of Oklahoma-Tulsa had adopted a diocese in Guatemala.

Initially there was nothing remarkable about Stan. There was even a touch of the Cure D'Ars about him. Like the famous French priest of the 19th Century, he too had struggled with the discipline of Latin and nearly failed to finish seminary. As a young priest – ordained in 1963 – he had served with little notice through his first five years, while moving among four different Oklahoma parishes. Then he volunteered for the foreign diocese with which his bishop had twinned.

It was particularly difficult for him to tackle the Mayan dialect of the Tzutuhil Indians. However, having passed this obstacle, he quickly won over the trust and respect of the people by his complete dedication to their needs. The pastoral work alone was overwhelming – the usual cycle of baptisms, marriages and funerals, the training of catechists and ministers of the Eucharist, the constant visits to the sick and the dying. And always there was a constant stream of people to his door, looking for help in the form of food or medicine. Sunday Masses were attended by 3,500 people every week.

And as if all this was not enough, Fr Stan could often be found wielding a hoe in a farmer's cornfield, or organising food cooperatives, or even weaving. As the years progressed, the parish became known as a centre of renewal and Stan was accepted into the inner circles of village life. The people even conferred on him a unique honour, given to no other American priest. He was called Padre A'Plas, which was an Indian name. He even translated the New Testament into the local dialect and would later boast 'I am now preaching in Tzutuhil.'

Stan could not imagine living anywhere else or being with any other group of people. Indeed his life and ministry seemed idyllic, far away from the turmoil of the wider political scene. The roots of this violence went back to the original Spanish conquest five hundred years before. However, a succession of military governments had found in a crusade of AntiCommunism a convenient excuse to use brutal force against any challenge to their authority and to the status quo. In the 1980s this violence reached as far as the Church itself.

Fr Stan had written at one time to his bishop:

the country here is in rebellion and the government is taking it out on the Church. The low wages that are paid, the very few who are excessively rich, the bad distribution of land – these are some of the reasons for widespread discontent. The Church seems to be the only force that is trying to do something about the situation, and therefore the government is after us.

Eventually the violence reached Santiago Atitlan. Stan and his pastoral team knew they would have to take precautions. However he himself resisted any suggestion that he return to the states. 'At the first sign of danger the shepherd can't run and leave the sheep to fend for themselves.' Yet one day one of Stan's leading catechists was captured in broad daylight in front of the church and tortured and killed. The man's screams haunted Stan and he was disturbed afterwards at his own inability to help him. Soon his own name appeared on a death list. He was persuaded that his presence was an actual danger to the remaining members of the pastoral team and so he decided reluctantly to return to his native America. Yet he could not bear to remain long away from them.

Fr Stan returned in time for Holy Week and was indeed looking forward to celebrating the great events of that week with his parishioners. The sufferings and death of Christ took on a deeper meaning against the backdrop of the violence and suffering of the people. However, in the middle of the night on July 28 1981, death came for the shepherd. Three masked men burst into Stan's presbytery. Later it was thought that their initial intention was to capture and torture him, perhaps thereby encouraging him to return to the States and stay there. However, the priest put up a fight and in the struggle the men shot him twice in the head. 'Kill me here', he was heard to cry. He was the tenth priest to die in Guatemala that year.

After the funeral, Stan's body was returned to his native Oklahoma, but his family agreed to the request of his parish and allowed his heart to be returned and interred in the church of Santiago Atitlan. His father Tom said: 'his heart belonged with those people. He loved them and they loved him. I think Stanley knew he could do far more for them in death than he ever did in life. I truly believe that is why he went back. He knew that was his purpose in life.'

GEORGES ROUAULT

For someone who could not draw or paint to save himself, I have been grateful to the Lord that He at least gave me a discerning appreciation for art and the work of artists! Art teachers may disagree with my self-diagnosis – I can think of one former colleague who claimed everyone could paint or draw, with a little help!

Yet who could not be moved by Michelangelo's Sistine ceiling, or the Pieta that stands in St Peter's Basilica? Who could remain untouched by Giotto's frescoes in Assisi, which feature the life of St Francis? Nowadays, even if we never actually visit these places, we can see them in television documentaries or even admire them on the internet. All of us can see the Divine print in the majesty of marble and colour and the hand of God in the hand of the artist.

Georges Rouault once said that his desire was to be able to paint Christ so movingly that those who saw Him would be converted. It was quite a claim and one that he probably came to realise on many occasions. He was born in Paris in May 1871 to a poor family, yet despite this he was encouraged by his mother in his love for the arts. At the age of fourteen, he was apprenticed as a glass painter and restorer and this experience no doubt influenced his later use of the heavy black contouring that featured in his paintings and characterised his later style. The apprenticeship was followed by a period of study at the École des Beaux Arts, where he found among his fellow students people like Henri Matisse and Henri Manguin among others. Georges was recognised as an accomplished and promising student.

Despite his personal gifts and accomplishments, Georges was unhappy. For all his skills he felt there was something missing. 'I know nothing of suffering' was how he put it. About the age of thirty there was a dramatic change in his artistic and religious perspectives. He wrote: 'I was seized with a sort of madness, or of grace, depending on one's perspective. The face of the world changed for me. I saw everything that I had seen before but in a different form and with a different harmony.' He had discovered Christ but in a new and totally fresh way. Was what happened akin to the vision of Thomas Aquinas, who afterwards could not write another word and saw all he had written before as 'so much straw'? Or was it like the stigmata of Francis on La Verna?

The first decades of the 20th century in France were heady days for the Church, with many significant conversions against a backdrop of great literary life. There were figures such as Charles Peguy and Francois Mauriac. Georges was particularly close to the Maritains, a couple who had come to Christianity as adults and who were to contribute so much to the philosophical life of the nation and the Church. The novelist Leon Bloy was also a friend, though not always one who affirmed the artist.

As Rouault developed his style, there were three areas or subjects which seemed to dominate – and they were very disparate – the brothel, the circus and the courtroom. Each offered an opportunity to reflect on the themes of judgement and hypocrisy and, in a sense, the human condition. Each could be linked into the passion of Christ. 'All of my work is religious,' wrote Rouault, 'for those who know how to look at it.' His Christian faith informed his work in his constant search for inspiration and marks him out as perhaps the most passionate Christian artist of the 20th century. The face of Jesus and the cries of the women at the foot of the cross are symbols – among others – for Rouault of the pain of the world, which for him was relieved by belief in the resurrection.

Indeed painting was for him a form of prayer, a dialogue between him and his savior. In 1948 he shared with the public his most personal work, a labour of love of over 20 years. It was entitled 'Miserere' and it was a series of 58 engravings based on the passion and death of Christ. In these pictures Rouault expressed the humanity of Christ in contrast to the inhumanity of his persecutors. 'We think ourselves kings, but we are more accurately seen as circus clowns, each wearing our own mask to disguise our true nature.' 'Are we not all convicts?' one title in the series asks. It is such a great work that some have even said it is a great contribution to the Christological debates of the century. Rouault had become so conscious of suffering and man's inhumanity to his fellow man – the labour began during the Great War – that he wrote 'what saves us from ourselves, if anything can, is Christ and the Virgin Mary.'

Sadly his work was slow to be appreciated in the official halls of the Church. Just as he stood apart from the secularised culture of the contemporary art world, so his dark and rough-hewn style of painting with its bold lines had little to do with the art so often found in the churches of his native land. At the end of his life he had destroyed 300 of his own pictures (estimated to be worth millions of euros today) simply because he did not feel that he would live long enough to finish them. It was only towards the end of this life that he was commissioned to produce three stain glass windows for a church in Assy. In keeping with the man, he refused any payment.

In 1953 Rouault was named a papal knight by Pope Pius XII, and he died five years later in Paris on February 13 1958.

JOAN SAWYER

The story of Joan Sawyer has simple and humble origins in a country village in Co Laois in 1932. Her parents, George and Brigid, moved then to Antrim in search of work. At that stage, they had three children and Joan was born some years after their move. Despite the fact that they were the only Catholic children at the school she remembers receiving only acceptance and love.

The family went to the local Catholic church, which was called St Comgall's. This was supplemented by the strong faith and example of their parents. Despite the fact that she had no contact with any religious order or sisters, by the age of sixteen, Joan felt 'there was something more' and that perhaps God was calling her to something. She was fortunate that the parish priest, Vincent Davey, had spent some years on the missions in Nigeria and believed that this young woman had a genuine vocation.

It so happened that two sisters were visiting the schools in the diocese of Down and Connor that year, and so Fr Vincent introduced the young Joan to them. They too were impressed by her and had no doubt about her missionary vocation. She began novitiate the following year and on April 22 1952 she made her first profession at the age of twenty. Five years later she made her final profession.

However, Joan was not immediately transported to a foreign shore, even though this was normally the life that a missionary sister expected. Her early years were spent in Ireland and it wasn't until 1971 that she went to the United States to help with the mission effort there. Still there was a restlessness in her, because so much of her time was spent at a desk and in an office. She yearned to be 'out in the field' and bringing the gospel to those who had never heard it.

She shared her anguish with her superior, and particularly about her great desire to go to Peru. And so it was in December 1977, at the age of forty-five, Sister Joan Sawyer stepped into the final chapter of her life. She arrived in Peru. Her heart was full of a great desire to meet people and share in their lives. She knew well how many lived in dire poverty and had poor housing and insufficient food and clothing.

Joan's first assignment was to the parish of Condevilla, an area of almost 100,000 people where there was incredible poverty and malnutrition. Against a backdrop of Liberation theology, she endeavoured to do what she could for the people, especially the women and children. She was criticised by some but she could never pass anyone by, her great desire being to let them know Christ loved them and cared for them. Soon there was basic schooling and food kitchens set up. Relief organisations were contacted to provide the material needs for the people.

But now another phase – and a final one – was to begin for Joan. She moved to the terrible prison of Lurigancho in Lima, which had been built ten years before for 1,800 men and now held 6,500. Conditions were awful with such overcrowding. Joan was assigned to one wing where 350 men lived. She got to know them and the addresses of their families. She acted as a liaison between them and their families outside, bringing food and clothes to the men and precious news to the relatives outside.

Despair was the order of the day but Joan tried to instill hope. She would pray with them if allowed and helped to organise the weekly Mass when the chaplain would come. She became a familiar figure in the Department of Justice, trying to ensure that the prisoners would get a trial and that time already spent in prison – sometimes long – would be taken into consideration. Indeed she was as good as any solicitor. Indeed it was on one such errand that she met her own final end.

It was December 1983 and Christmas was approaching. It would be a time when the authorities could be leaned on to let some prisoners home for the holiday period, and maybe even for good.

She set out one morning carrying with her a small jar of food from a mother and some money, which she had been given to help pay for legal aid. She performed the tasks and was on her way out when she stopped at the chaplaincy door. Her prisoner guide knocked on the door, and Joan entered to find three other sisters there – and nine prisoners. This was the day that the latter had decided to escape and Joan had inadvertently stumbled on their plan. All four sisters were now 'hostages' as the men and the authorities negotiated a safe passage for all concerned.

At five o'clock, the negotiation ended and they were allowed to enter an ambulance. Joan sat near the back door, but as soon as the van left the prison grounds the shooting started. Machine guns were used, and even though the police knew there were innocent hostages on board the van, they kept firing. The carnage was almost total – seven of the prisoners were dead, and Joan who had been hit by five bullets drew her last breath as the door of the ambulance was opened.

Cardinal Landazuri of Lima with eighty priests concelebrated the funeral Mass and expressed his and the people's indignation at the injustice that had been perpetrated. Perhaps the most poignant words came from Julio, the young man to whom Joan had brought the money from his mother:

minutes before Sister Juanita was taken hostage I was speaking with her when she came with a package sent by my mother. I can still see her eyes, which reached to eternity. Her love, pure and gentle, which reflected her great love for people. Her spirit of kindness and sacrifice towards us prisoners will be my most precious memory.

In the legal aftermath there were some minor sentences handed down but to this day no one has been convicted of the death of Sister Joan and the seven prisoners. The cross still stands there marking the spot where she met her end. A message reads simply *'no mataras'* (Do not kill) It is a fitting tribute.

SOPHIE AND HANS SCHOLL

Readers will recall how firmly Pope Benedict addressed the issue of the 'new atheism' and modern political correctness when he made his pilgrimage to England and Scotland in September 2010. He reminded his listeners that the Nazi regime under which he suffered had tried to deny the presence of God in the life of his own nation. It was a challenging link, which no doubt made many people sit up and take note even if they did not agree with his words.

The people remembered in this article would have identified with the Pope's words. In the summer of 1942 the citizens of Munich – where Josef Ratzinger was briefly archbishop in the 1970s – were astonished by a series of leaflets, which began to circulate throughout the city. Slipped into mailboxes by unknown hands, left in empty bus stops or on park benches, the leaflets contained a sweeping indictment of the Nazi regime and called on their readers to work for the defeat of their own nation. At a time when the merest hint of dissent was an act of treason, the boldness of this open call to resistance threw the Gestapo, the Nazi secret police, into a rage.

Although raised as Lutherans, Hans and Sophie Scholl had been initially stirred into action by reading the courageous sermons of a Catholic bishop, Cardinal Clemens Von Galen, the 'Lion of Munster', who denounced the euthanasia policies of the Nazi regime, whereby the lives of many mentally retarded and 'infirm' people were deliberately and systematically ended. Several of the Scholls' pamphlets also described the mass executions and deportations of the Jews to the death camps. Such free speech was forbidden in Germany as it was felt it undermined the war effort. An interesting footnote also to this period was the fact that Sophie sent two volumes of the sermons of Cardinal John Henry Newman – beatified by Pope Benedict in September 2010 – to her boyfriend who was a soldier on the Russian front.

Contrary to the initial suspicions of the authorities this work was not that of any sophisticated organisation or any external body. They were in fact a few dozen university students who had been inspired by their Christian faith and the idealism of youth to challenge the brutal and tyrannical regime that held sway in Germany at that time. At the centre of the group were a brother and sister, Hans and Sophie Scholl, who were twenty-four and twenty-one years old respectively. Hans was a medical student and his sister studied philosophy. They had no other weapons than their courage, the power of truth and an illegal duplicating machine.

Hans in fact had originally enlisted in the German army but one day he saw a young Jewish woman under forced labour digging a trench. He reached down to give her a flower but she saw only a Nazi and she rejected his offer. This moment was crucial in his own 'conversion', and when he returned to medical school he moved further to the cause of truth and freedom. Sophie too had been an exemplary German citizen and initially a leader in a Nazi youth group. At university the brother and sister found others of like mind who were drawn together by a shared love of music and literature, as well as hiking in the local Bavarian mountains. A question they often pondered was how the individual must act under a dictatorship.

Hans and Sophie were devout Christians: members of the Lutheran Church. They believed that the struggle in which they were engaged was a battle for the very soul of Germany and thus a duty for all Christians. One of their leaflets read:

> Everywhere and at all times of greatest trial, men have appeared, prophets and saints who cherished their freedom, who preached the One God and who with His help brought the people to a reversal of their downward course. Man is free, to be sure, but without the true God he is defenceless against the principle of evil… we must attack evil where it is strongest, and it is strongest in the power of Hitler… we will not be silent. We are your bad conscience. The White Rose will not leave you in peace.

As their campaign continued, their boldness grew. Soon graffiti appeared on walls – 'Down with Hitler' – on street signs and the sides of buildings. However, this group of amateurs must have known that their efforts would be short-lived. On February 18 1943 Hans and Sophie were caught distributing leaflets outside a lecture hall in the university and were arrested. Jacob Schmidt, the university handyman and Nazi party member, saw the Scholls with their leaflets and reported them. Under arrest, they bravely confessed to all the actions of the 'White Rose' (a name they took from a Spanish novel) in order to try and spare some of the other members of the group. Despite their efforts the Gestapo quickly rounded up the other conspirators in the circle both in Munich and Hamburg where there was a sister group.

There was a trial but the verdict was a foregone conclusion. The judge scarcely listened to their arguments and so the brother and sister along with a third man, Christophe Probst, also a medical student, were sentenced to death. On her way to sentencing, Sophie's mother turned to her and said: 'You know, Sophie, Jesus' and the daughter nodded in agreement. Just a few days later they were executed by guillotine and the sentence was all the more cruel in that they each had to lie on their back without a blindfold and see the falling blade before it struck.

Understandably it has taken Germany time to recover psychologically from the memories of the war. However, in a poll in 2003, a television station invited viewers to vote for their ten most important Germans of all time. Hans and Sophie were catapulted into fourth place ahead of Bach and Goethe and even Albert Einstein. The 'White Rose' has not been forgotten.

ROGER SCHUTZ

It was a culture shock at first. Twenty-two years ago I brought a group of fifty young people from our northern diocese to the village of Taize in France. The wooden pallets for beds, the simple food and the 'interesting' toilets challenged our pampered bodies – but the babble of languages and the spirit of prayer which permeated the place lifted our spirits, despite ourselves. And then there was Frere Roger.

We saw him sitting at the front of the brothers as they meandered in to the huge chapel after the bell had tolled to summon us all to prayer. The brothers took their prayer seriously – three times a day – and they took time at it. The chapel highlighted the different emphases of the three main Christian groups – the icons for the Orthodox, the Eucharistic presence for the Catholic and the Word for the Protestant.

Roger sat and prayed silently, a magnet for our eyes and our thoughts. Sometimes after a meeting he would mingle among the many hundreds of young people and sometimes he would meet a smaller group – usually from one country – over a cup of Taize tea. Always he was genial and gracious, a smile never absent from his serene face. You knew you were in the presence of a saint.

But who was Brother Roger? He had been born in 1915, the son of a Lutheran pastor and a French Protestant mother. His own interest in spiritual matters began at an early stage. When he was twenty-five, he visited the little village of Taize with the idea of founding a Protestant monastic community. He had already been attracted by the ideals and work of St Benedict.

Roger bought two derelict houses and used them to help the victims of the war, which was raging at the time. It was a perilous location so close to the border between Occupied France and the part that was free. He even at one time had to flee from the Gestapo. However, he returned in 1944 with some other like-minded men and set up a community. He said at that time, 'I discovered my Christian identity by reconciling within myself my Protestant origins and my faith in the Catholic Church'.

Five years later, the brothers would take their first monastic vows and Roger drew up the first rule of Taize, which was summed up in the words: 'Preserve at all times an interior silence to live in Christ's presence and cultivate the spirit of the Beatitudes – joy, simplicity and mercy.' Although the community was regarded with suspicion by the mainstream Churches, its numbers grew from twelve in 1950 to sixty-five in 1965 and to more than 100 members today.

In 1969, Cardinal Marty, head of the French bishops, authorised Catholics to join it. Cardinal Angelo Roncalli, nuncio in France and later Pope John XXIII, visited the community on one occasion and spoke warmly of 'that little springtime'. When he became Pope, he invited Roger and another brother, the theologian Max Thurian, to attend the Second Vatican Council. Pope John Paul visited Taize in 1986, compelled, as he put it, by 'an interior need'.

What was special about Roger? All his life he devoted himself to the reconciliation of the Churches. Part of his appeal may have been his dislike of formal preaching while encouraging a spiritual quest as a common endeavour. For instance, during one Taize gathering in Paris in 1995, he spoke to almost 10,000 young people who were sitting on the floor of a great exhibition hall. 'We have come here to search,' he said, 'to go on searching through silence and prayer, to get in touch with our inner life.' The winter gatherings became a feature of the Taize 'style', as thousands would meet in one or other of the capitals of Europe and engage a theme of prayer and reflection. Rome, Paris and Berlin were never quite the same after 20,000 to 25,000 young people descended on their streets and sang and danced their way to the various meeting points. Roger's own charism of creating beautiful language and moving prayers enabled the Taize newsletter, which preceded each winter or summer event, to be a source of inspiration for so many.

Sadly, as we know, Roger's life was to end tragically. On August 16 2005, in full view of 2,500 horrified young pilgrims, he was stabbed during the evening prayer service by a young schizophrenic woman from Romania. He died shortly afterwards.

Cardinal Walter Kasper, president of the Vatican's Council for Christian Unity, concelebrated the requiem Mass with four other priests of the community. 'Yes, the springtime of ecumenism has flowered on the hill of Taize,' he said in his sermon. The community had already forgiven the young woman.

Roger's successor, Br Alois, echoed all their sentiments: 'With Christ on the cross we say to you, Father, forgive her, she does not know what she did.'

The community of Taize continues to thrive, still attracting hundreds of thousands of young people from across the continent of Europe and beyond. It remains a testimony to the young man who came there in 1940, a man with Protestant roots, an Orthodox vision and a Catholic heart.

Maria Skobtsova

'Europe must breathe with two lungs', Pope John Paul used to remind people in the West, years before the fall of the Berlin wall and the opening up of the Iron Curtain. As a Slav he knew this. He even reminded Prime Minister Gorbachev when they met for the first time in the Vatican in 1989. The Communist leader understood this better than others. The history of Europe was not just about the events of France and Germany, Spain and Portugal. Since 1989 we have been learning of the heroes and heroines of the faith and of the many who gave their lives for the sake of the Gospel. They are giants of faith and courage – Edith Stein, Titus Brandsma, Jerzy Popiełuszko to name but a few. Soon John Paul will be raised to the altars and become one of those hero saints.

The story of Maria Skobtsova is one of these stories. It is a story in three acts, each with its own drama and narrative. In the beginning, she was born Elizabeth Pilenko into a prosperous Russian family. She was a distinguished poet and a committed political activist who married twice – once to a Bolshevik whom she soon divorced and later to an anti-Bolshevik from whom she separated. In the early stages of the Communist revolution she served as mayor of her hometown and in so doing risked the wrath of both left and right.

However, in 1923, she left all this and joined the myriads of people leaving Russia to make her way to Paris with her three young children. Sadly her youngest child, Anastasia, died of meningitis and this event caused a real conversion in Elizabeth's heart. She resolved to seek 'a more authentic and purified life... to be a mother of all, for all who need maternal care and protection.'

In Paris she became deeply involved with the many Russian refugees who had flocked to the city. She sought them out in hospitals and prisons as well as in mental asylums and the slums. Her own deep faith came to the fore, seeing in every person 'the very icon of God incarnate in the world.' Her own bishop encouraged her to become a nun, but she would only do this if she could be free to develop a new type of monasticism, that was engaged with the world, and that did not allow any 'barrier, which might separate the heart from the world and its wounds.'

In 1932, she finally made her religious profession and became Mother Maria Skobtsova. Thus began the second 'act' of her incredible life. Yet for her there was no hidden cloister or monastic enclosure. She took a lease on a simple house in the city and turned it into a refuge for those who were destitute. It was big enough to contain a chapel and a soup kitchen, but her own bed was a cot in the basement beside the boiler. 'At the Last Judgment I shall not be asked whether I was successful in my ascetic exercises, nor how many bows and prostrations I made. Instead I shall be asked, did I feed the hungry, clothe the naked, visit the sick and the prisoners.'

However something else was going on too, one could say equivalent to the Catholic Workers' Movement in the United States with Dorothy Day and Peter Maurin. Maria's house became a focal point for discussion and the renewal of the Orthodox faith. While her kitchen was crowded with the poor and hungry, her living room was full of the leading intellectuals of the day. Orthodox Action was born and as Maria explained 'the meaning of the liturgy must be translated into life. It is why Christ came into the world and why he gave us the liturgy.'

The third and shortest act of Maria's life was to enfold with the German occupation of Paris in 1940. Her work was seen by the Nazis as subversive. She and her chaplain, Fr Dimitri Klepinin, not only gave hospitality to Jews but also tried to hide them and help them escape the clutches of the Gestapo. These efforts continued until 1943 when they were arrested. Fr Dimitri and Maria's son Yuri died in Buchenwald concentration camp, and she herself was sent to Ravensbruck.

Here Maria managed to live for almost two years in indescribable conditions. Though stripped of her habit she remained the mother who strengthened the faith and courage of her fellow prisoners, helping to keep alive the spark of humanity, which the Nazi system tried to suffocate. 'I am your message, Lord.'

In light of the redemptive suffering of Christ, she was able to find a meaning in her own suffering. 'My state at present is such that I completely accept suffering in the knowledge that this is how things ought to be for me, and if I am to die I see in this a blessing from on high.'

In her final days, close as she was death, she performed one last heroic act, which summed up so beautifully her incredible spirituality. With a needle and thread, which she had purchased at the price of her meager bread ration, she embroidered an icon of Mary holding the infant Jesus, the child already bearing the wounds of the cross.

On the eve of Easter, March 31 1945 – and just days before the liberation of the camp by Russian troops – Maria gave her life in the gas chamber of Ravensbruck. She took the place of a Jewish woman. The day suitably was Holy Saturday, 1945. Maria is honoured at Yad Vashem, the Holocaust memorial in Jerusalem, as one of the 'Righteous of the Nations'. She was also glorified (canonised) a saint in the Orthodox tradition on January 16 2004, fittingly in the Cathedral of St Alexander Nevsky in Paris.

EDITH STEIN

'I picked a book at random and took out a large volume. It bore the title, *The Life of St Teresa of Avila*. I began to read, was at once captivated, and did not stop till I had reached the end. As I closed the book – it was already dawn – I said, "This is the truth".'

The following day, the reader went to the local church and asked to be baptised. The elderly priest asked her, 'How long have you been taking instruction?' 'Please, Father,' she replied, 'test my knowledge.' And he did, extensively. At the end, the priest was astonished by her accurate answers and, on New Year's Day 1922, Edith Stein was baptised into the Catholic faith. She chose Teresa as her baptismal name, and later that day she received the Eucharist for the first time.

The road to faith in Jesus Christ was not an easy one for Edith. The youngest in her family, she was born into the Jewish faith on October 12 1891, in the German city of Breslau, now Wrocław in Poland. Her father died when she was young, and her mother, Auguste, raised her seven children and ran the family timber business, even into her eighties. She was an impressive woman, who was proud of her Jewish traditions and faith.

By the age of twenty-one, Edith was a self-confessed atheist. To placate her mother, she continued to attend the synagogue, but she felt nothing there. In the meantime, she had excelled at her studies, and in 1916, after completing her doctoral thesis in philosophy, she became assistant to the great professor of phenomenonology, Edmund Husserl.

It was while she was with Husserl that Edith received the first jolt to her convinced atheism. A friend of hers, Adolf Reinach, a fellow philosopher at Gottingen, had died, and his widow had requested Edith to sort out his papers. Edith got a profound shock when she discovered how this Christian woman accepted the cross of Adolf's death.

Later Edith wrote, 'It was then that I first encountered the cross and the divine strength which it inspires in those who bear it. It was the moment in which my unbelief was shattered. Christ streamed out upon me: Christ in the mystery of the cross.'

It was at Gottingen also that she came into contact with Hedwig Conrad-Martius and his wife. It was in their house, one night when they had gone out to a function, that Edith picked up the volume of St Teresa's life and began to read. Hedwig later stood for her at her baptism.

Shortly after this event, Edith knew she could not keep her secret from her mother, and told her, 'Mother, I am a Catholic'. Auguste wept, and Edith with her. Later, a friend wrote about Auguste at this time, 'As a God-fearing woman, she sensed without realising it the holiness radiating from her daughter and, though her suffering was excruciating, she clearly recognised her helplessness before the mystery of grace'.

Edith spent the next few years at the Dominican convent in Speyer. There she taught German in exchange for a room and the meagre convent food. 'She quickly won the hearts of her pupils,' a sister wrote about her. 'In humility and simplicity almost unheard and unnoticed, she went quietly about her duties, always serenely friendly and accessible to anyone who wanted her help.' The world outside also wanted Edith. Her scholarship had not gone unnoticed, and so she went out regularly to give lectures to an appreciative public.

Lectures, publications and other work continued to multiply but, in the midst of it all, a life of deep prayer was growing. 'There is no sense in rebelling against it,' she wrote. 'It is merely necessary that one should, in fact, have a silent corner in which to converse with God, as if nothing else existed, every day.'

By late 1932, the situation was becoming more and more difficult in Germany, especially for Jews. In January 1933, Hitler came to power and set up the Third Reich. The Nazis began to pass laws, which were designed to marginalise non-Aryans from public life. On February 23 1933, Edith gave her last lecture.

As one door closed, another seemed inexorably to open. The desire for religious life, which she had felt for years, now began to flourish. In May 1933, she visited the Carmel in Cologne, and on October 14, the eve of the feast of St Teresa, her baptismal patron, she entered the convent.

The famous philosopher and lecturer now became the novice. Her tastes had always been simple, but now her little cell, no more than ten feet square, contained nothing but a straw mattress, a water jug, a few unframed pictures of Carmelite saints, and a plain wooden cross on the wall. Such was the décor of a Carmelite cell. Here was the battleground where daily the nun struggled against her own self-interest until her nature was wedded to grace.

On April 15 1934, Edith was clothed in the habit, and took the name she herself had suggested, Sr Teresa Benedicta of the Cross. The following year, on Easter Sunday, she made her profession. 'How do you feel?' someone asked. 'Like the bride of the Lamb!' was her reply.

If 1935 brought much joy, the following year brought sorrow. Initially, her mother had not returned Edith's weekly letters. In time, however, Edith learned that Auguste had begun to visit a local Carmel secretly, and soon she began to write to her daughter. There was not a lot of time, however, for Auguste died later that year, but Edith was so glad that mother and daughter had become reconciled before the end came.

As the Nazis gained a stranglehold on the life of the nation, the situation in Germany continued to deteriorate. A decision was made that Edith and Rosa, her sister who had followed her into the Church and Carmel, should leave Cologne and move to Echt in Holland. Holland too was in the grip of the Nazis, however, and many Jews were being deported to the concentration camps established by the Nazis – and to certain death.

In July 1942, the Dutch bishops issued a letter condemning the treatment of the Jews. They urged the faithful to examine their consciences, and to pray for divine help. The German authorities were displeased at the bishops' audacity, and on August 2, all non-Aryan people were arrested. It was a reprisal for the letter, the German commissar said.

That very afternoon, two SS officers arrived at the convent, and Edith was arrested, together with Rosa. From Echt, she was brought to Auschwitz extermination camp, in Poland. She never returned: for her life, and Rosa's, ended there on August 9 1942, just a few days after their arrest.

Even in those terrible final days, however, she had work to do. A Jewish businessman who knew her in the camp wrote later, 'Sr Benedicta at once took charge of the poor little ones, washed and combed them, and saw to it that they got food and attention'. Another fellow prisoner said, 'She was thinking of the sorrow she foresaw: not her own sorrow – for that she was far too calm – but the sorrow that awaited others. Her whole appearance suggested only one thought to me: a *pieta* without Christ'.

Today, Auschwitz stands pristine in its condition, preserved as a museum by the Polish nation, as if frozen in time from the moment the Nazi guards left it. It is a painful reminder to the world of the evil power of racism. Like the millions of others, no stone marks Edith's grave.

In 1998, Pope John Paul canonised her as a saint, with a feast on the ninth of August. On that occasion, the Pope said:

> The modern world boasts of the enticing door, which says everything is permitted. It ignores the narrow gate of discernment and renunciation.
>
> I am speaking to you, young Christians. Your life is not an endless series of open doors! Listen to your heart! Do not stay on the surface, but go to the heart of things! And when the time is right, have the courage to decide! The Lord is waiting for you to put your freedom in his good hands.

Edith would surely have added 'This is the truth'!

ALOYSIUS STEPINAC

You may have seen his picture on a wall. Visitors to Medjugorje in recent years will have stopped off for a break from the long journey from airport to shrine. Perhaps a Mass followed by some refreshment was the order of the day. Invariably when the pilgrims entered the Croatian church, the picture of Aloysius Stepinac was there. To many Croats he remains a hero, someone who stood for them against the Communist regime, which so dominated their politics for decades after the Second World War. His story begins a bit earlier.

In July 1931 a young priest returned to his native town in order to celebrate his first Mass at home after his ordination in Rome. The parish priest said to Barbara, his mother, that she could finally end her years of fasting and self-denial. 'Absolutely not,' replied the woman. 'I'll pray the rosary and fast even more now so that my son might become a saintly priest.'

Aloysius Stepinac (Alojzije in his native Croatian) was the young man in question and he did indeed go on to become a saintly priest. Born in May 1898 he completed his military training and indeed served his country with distinction before going to study for the priesthood. He was an extremely bright student and while residing in the Pontifical German College in Rome he took doctoral studies at the Gregorian University and was ordained on October 26 1930.

There was a brief period of pastoral experience as a priest in the city of Zagreb. But in 1936, barely six years after ordination to the priesthood, he was made coadjutor archbishop of Zagreb and the following year he succeeded as archbishop when his predecessor died. The date was December 7 1937.

The storm clouds were gathering over Europe. Nazism was growing at a phenomenal rate in Germany and in its satellite states. Fascism was rife in other lands of Europe, including his own and, of course, Communism was always the great threat in the East. The Church was certainly caught – it was difficult to choose or even be seen to choose.

Initially Aloysius had been optimistic about the Church's position when Ante Pavelic and the Utasha regime had come to power. Pavelic had seemed a positive alternative to the godless supporters of Communism. On April 10 each year he would celebrate a Mass to celebrate the proclamation of the Ustase state.

But soon he was appalled by the Fascist policies of the government and protested against their treatment of Jews and Serbs and gypsies. In May 1942 he stated in a diocesan letter 'all men and all races are children of God: all without distinction. Those who are gypsies, black, European or Aryan all have the same rights... for this reason the Catholic Church had always condemned and continues to condemn all injustice and all violence committed in the name of theories of class, race or nationality.'

When the Second World War was in its full throes, desperate measures were often required. Stepinac was particularly concerned for those who were Jewish or Orthodox in faith. To save as many as possible he allowed his priests to accept as a convert any Jew or Orthodox Christian without the requirement of special catechetical knowledge and with the understanding that they would return to their own faiths 'when these times of madness and savageness are over.' The chief Rabbi of Zagreb, the capital city, spoke of Stepinac as 'truly blessed' since he did the best he could during the war.

The end of one chapter, however, came when the Communists

triumphed in what was to be called Yugoslavia ('all the Slavs') and Stepinac was put under great pressure by the new ruler, Joseph Tito, to create a nationalised Catholic Church, independent from Rome. This he refused to do and so began to pay the price – vilified in the press, ridiculed by Communist spokesmen and even made the target of hate campaigns.

In October 1945 he published a letter in which he outlined the numbers of priests killed or imprisoned since the change of regime. Arrested on the spurious charges of war crimes, he was put on trial in September 1946 and sentenced on October 11 to sixteen years of hard labour for defending the Holy See and the Church. He could have left the country – the Communists would have preferred he did so – but Stepinac wished to remain with the people. When Tito released him after five years of imprisonment, again he had the option of going to Rome but he chose to stay under house arrest in his home parish of Krasic.

He was imprisoned until 1951 when his health was beginning to seriously deteriorate. Even during this time, he managed to write over 5,000 letters to people all over the country, and within the confines of the prison he ministered as best he could as a priest.

On June 23 1953, Pope Pius XII made Stepinac a cardinal, citing him 'as an example of apostolic zeal and Christian strength.' Yugoslavia retaliated by breaking diplomatic ties with the Vatican. On June 2 1959 he wrote a letter to a close friend: 'I likely will not live to see the collapse of Communism in the world due to my poor health. But I am absolutely certain of that collapse.' Aloysius remained under house arrest after his release from prison and he died on February 10 1960, almost certainly as a result of poisoning by the Communist authorities.

The Catholic Church declared Stepinac a martyr in November 1997 and on October 3 1998 Pope John Paul II declared him – before half a million Croats – a Blessed of the Church. Aloysius had indeed become a 'saintly priest.'

CORRIE TEN BOOM

The corner shop was like a million others scattered throughout Holland or any other part of Europe. A small family business had been started there – repairing watches – in 1837 and it had passed from father to son by the beginning of the Second World War. Casper Ten Boom was a good worker, conscientious and caring. He lived here with his two unmarried daughters, Corrie and Betsie, and through the decades they were active in social work in the local area. Their house was always open for anyone in need. They were devout Christians – members of the Dutch Reformed Church.

When the Great War came, Holland was very quickly overrun by the Nazi war machine and very soon the Ten Boom house became a refuge and hiding place for those who were fleeing from the Nazis. It was their non-violent way of resisting the German forces and it led them to hide Jews, students who refused to cooperate with the Nazis, and members of the Dutch underground movement. Corrie credited her father's example in inspiring her to help the Jews of Holland. In one incident, she recorded that she had asked a pastor who was visiting their home to help shield a mother and newborn infant: "'Definitely not,' he replied. "We could lose our lives for that Jewish child!" Unseen by either of us my father had appeared in the doorway. "Give the child to me Corrie." He held the child close, his white beard brushing the baby's cheeks. "You say we could lose our lives for this child. I would consider that the greatest honour that could come to my family.'"

During 1943 and into 1944, there were never less than six or seven people illegally living in their home – four Jews and two or three members of the underground. Additional refugees would stay with the family for a few hours or a few days until another 'safe house' could be located. Corrie, this quiet and rather plain spinster, became the ringleader within the Haarlem network and it was estimated that the network saved more than 800 Jews by the end of the war. On a daily basis she found herself dealing with hundreds of stolen ration cards to feed the Jews who were hiding in places all over Holland. Often she wondered how long this clandestine activity could continue.

On February 28 1944, the family was betrayed by an informer, and the Gestapo, the Nazi secret police, raided their home. They had set a trap and during the day they seized everyone who came to the house – in all 30 people were captured and within a few hours Corrie and her father and sister found themselves in prison. Yet somehow the Gestapo could not find what they were looking for – the hiding place which was located behind a false wall in the home. Its six occupants remained hidden for almost two days without water and food but somehow they survived, and of the four Jews three made it to the end of the war.

The Ten Booms were taken to Scheveningen prison and old Casper only lasted 10 days before he died. When he was asked if he knew he would be imprisoned for hiding Jews he replied 'it would be an honour to give my life for God's ancient people.' The two sisters then spent 10 months in three different prisons, finally ending up in the notorious Ravensbruck camp near Berlin. Life there was horrendous, but Corrie and Betsie spent their time sharing their deep faith and love with their fellow prisoners. Many women became Christians in that terrible place because of the witness of the two sisters. It was their 'finest hour' as Corrie later described in her book 'The Hiding Place'.

At the beginning the sisters were afraid to share their faith, but as the nights went by and no guard visited their barrack they began to take the lead in prayer and sharing of scripture. 'These were evenings like no other. A single meeting might include a recital of the Magnificat by the Catholics, a whispered hymn by Lutherans and a sotto voce chant by the Orthodox.' Then Corrie or Betsie would open their smuggled Bible and read a text in Dutch and someone would translate into German or French or Russian, and the word of God echoed around the beams in a dozen different languages. 'It was truly a Pentecost moment.'

Sadly, Betsie died in the camp but Corrie survived the war and realised that she had to share what Betsie and herself had learnt in the camp: 'there is no pit so deep that God's love is not deeper still' Betsie would say. 'God will give us the love to forgive our enemies.' She made her way back to Haarlem and tried to pick up the watch mending trade again but her heart wasn't in it. At the age of 53, Corrie then began a ministry, which took her to over 60 countries over the next 33 years. Often she would speak of how God's love could overcome even the greatest evil, which was personified in the Nazi terror. On one occasion she even met one of the guards who had whipped her sister in the camp. He heard her speak of this love and of God's forgiveness, and after the meeting he approached Corrie and extended his hand. She recognised him and immediately she struggled with her own hatred for what he had done to Betsie. Somehow she was able to take his hand in hers and offer him the forgiveness he sought.

In her latter years, Corrie emigrated to the United States and lived in the state of California. In her last years she experienced a series of debilitating strokes. 'The tramp for the Lord' had served her Master in health; now she was being called to serve Him in illness. It was like a second imprisonment. Yet despite her inability to speak she was able to remain joyful and full of hope for everyone who came to visit her. She died at the age of 91 in 1983.

Engelmar Unzeitig

A young boy dreamt of doing great things for God – of going to far off lands and becoming a missionary priest – to dedicate his life to 'the conversion of pagans.' He got his wish, but not quite as he expected.

Engelmar Unzeitig was born in a German area of what was then Czechoslovakia in 1911 and entered a missionary order when he was just 17. The usual programme of studies led to ordination on August 15 1939. Two weeks later war broke out, and within a short time he was arrested by the Gestapo for 'the unpardonable sin' of defending the Jews in his sermons. By June 1941, he found himself in the concentration camp of Dachau, which was near Munich. He had found his mission field even if it was somewhat nearer than his boyhood dream. '*Arbeit macht frei*' the sign above the entrance said. 'Work makes you free'. Engelmar would put this into practice over the next few years.

There are few left who remember personally the atrocities of the Nazis and the great crime of the Holocaust when almost six million Jews perished into the camps across Poland and Germany. Most of us read about these things in history books. It is fitting that we do not forget or dismiss this great blot on the conscience of mankind. It is hard to believe that even today there are some who try to 'airbrush' the Holocaust as if it never happened.

What we may not always remember is that there were many others who died in those camps and many of these were priests. Perhaps Maximilian Kolbe is the most famous, along with others like Titus Brandsma, but the story of Fr Engelmar who served most of his priesthood in Dachau deserves not to be forgotten.

During the war, most of the Jews who perished were sent to Poland. There the chimneys operated constantly from 1942, far from the sight and smell of the German people. But the camp at Dachau was on German soil, and while it was not an extermination camp like Auschwitz or Treblinka, many died within its barbed wire and its squalid conditions.

At one point there would have been up to two hundred thousand inmates from forty countries. Many of these were clergymen who had dared to defy the ruling Nazi ethos. They were held in special contempt by the SS and segregated in the 'priests' barracks'. With good reason, it was rightly called the 'largest monastery in the world'. There amid the starvation and filth and atmosphere of death, the priests and other clergymen sang and prayed and where possible celebrated Mass. Above all they tried to offer a pastoral service to all the other prisoners who valued their ministry in the midst of such squalor.

For the newly ordained priest, Dachau was almost his first pastoral experience. Despite the horrendous conditions, he tried to regard it as a school for holiness. In a letter smuggled out to his sister, he wrote: 'What sometimes appears as misfortune is often the greatest fortune. How much a person learns only through experience in the school of life.'

Engelmar was not treated any differently from the other prisoners. To his Nazi captors, he was simply a prisoner. So he too had to engage in forced labour and work in the horrific cold and damp of the camp. Like the others, he managed to survive on the meager rations. A 'meal' of grass and weeds could seem like a feast to a starving stomach. Yet in so far as he could, he tried to minister to the other men.

Somehow this young priest managed to last for four years in Dachau, and would probably have lasted to the end of the war except for an outbreak of typhus in the winter of 1945. In January of that year, nearly three thousand prisoners died from the disease. A special barracks was built to house those infected. A call went out for volunteer orderlies. Twenty priests stepped forward and Engelmar was one of them. The men knew it was a virtual death sentence, for those who entered the barracks had little chance of returning. Conditions there were terrible – lice and fleas were everywhere, the floor was awash with the blood and spit and waste of the dying. Within the Hell of Dachau, this was indeed the inner sanctum.

Nevertheless the priests entered and did their best to ease the final days and hours of the men – they washed their bodies, cleaned their pallets and tried to feed them with the meager rations provided. Above all they heard confessions and offered the last rites to those who requested them. The SS would certainly not enter this area and so they were able to exercise their ministry without fear.

Of the twenty-eight volunteers who entered, only two survived and Engelmar was not one of them. Within six weeks of entering, his own body was burning with fever and he knew he had contracted the deadly disease.

Still he continued to hear confessions and administer the sacraments as long as he was able. He died on March 2 1945, a few days after his thirty-fourth birthday, and just a few weeks before the camp was liberated by American troops. His ashes were smuggled out and later buried in the cemetery at Wurzburg and then later transferred to the order's church in the town.

In a letter written a few days before his death, Engelmar said: 'The Good is undying and victory must remain with God, even if it sometimes seems useless for us to spread love in the world. Nevertheless, one sees again and again that the human heart is attuned to love, and it cannot withstand its power in the long run, if it is truly based on God and not on creatures.'

In 1991 the process for beatification was begun, and in 2000 Engelmar was declared a 'martyr of the Church'.

SIMONE WEIL

It must be forty years ago now but I remember well the first time I heard the name of Simone Weil. The philosophy lecturer was obviously a fan. There was something about this bright young woman who chose to live a deeply spiritual life and yet to do so – seemingly – outside the Church, which appealed to the radical in him. I too was intrigued.

There was indeed something saintly and heroic in the life of this French Jewess. Born in 1909 her parents were well educated but non-religious. They recognised that their daughter was exceptional – she had learnt classical Greek by the age of twelve – and they ensured that she had the best of educations. She studied philosophy at the elite École Superieur in preparation for a teaching career, but her interests ranged over many fields – including literature, history, politics and mathematics. Her only brother, Andre, was one of the great mathematicians of the century.

After graduation, she taught in a number of schools and somehow divided her time between teaching and working as an activist in the local trade union movement. She had a great sense of sharing the experience of the working class and this led to her volunteering in the Spanish Civil war, where she worked with a French anarchist brigade. Simone was really not cut out to be a soldier, and her clumsiness repeatedly put her comrades at risk. In the end, her life was probably spared by an accidental injury, which meant her returning to France.

It was this sense of sharing completely in the lives of others that marked Simone so much. Even at the age of six, she had given up sugar in solidarity with the troops entrenched along the Western front in the Great War. It was this identification that had driven her to Spain and the civil war. However, after this in the late 1930s, she had another experience, which reinforced her spiritual inclinations. Once, while watching a religious procession in a tiny Portuguese fishing village and hearing the beautiful singing, she felt the conviction arise within her 'that Christianity is pre-eminently the religion of slaves, that slaves cannot help belonging to it and I among others.' Later in a chapel in the Italian town of Assisi, she felt the need for the first time to get down on her knees in prayer.

However, it was in 1938 that she had the experience that 'marked her forever'. She had been spending Holy Week in the Benedictine monastery in Solesmes. At the time she was suffering from a headache, a condition to which she was prone. That evening in the chapel in the quiet darkness she was reciting the poem 'Love' by the English poet George Herbert and she felt a tremendous identification with the pain of the suffering Christ. In this effort she felt that 'Christ himself came down and took possession of me.'

Simone returned to her study of philosophy and science but now her radical vision was trained on the meaning of God's intervention into history through the incarnation and the cross of Christ. She immersed herself in the New Testament, and also in attending Mass. She studied the mystic writers like John of the Cross and Teresa of Avila. She brought herself to the very threshold of faith, and yet she did not cross the river of baptism.

Nothing that was Catholic or even Christian was alien to her, and yet she chose not to be baptised, convinced as she was of a vocation to be a Christian outside the Church. 'I cannot help wondering whether in these days when so large a proportion of humanity is submerged in materialism, God does not want there to be some men and women who have given themselves to him and to Christ and who yet remain outside the Church.' Again it was a harking back to that total identification with the poor and the suffering. She could not bear the thought of separating herself from the 'immense and unfortunate multitude of unbelievers.'

In 1940, Simone was fired as a Jew from her teaching position by the Vichy government. She went with her family to harvest grapes in the countryside around Marseilles. Then in 1942 she left and went to America. Here she is known to have attended daily Mass in Corpus Christi Church in Harlem, where the future Trappist monk Thomas Merton would be received into the Church. There is recent evidence too – including a claim from a priest who knew her – that she herself sought and received Baptism just before her death.

However, soon she was feeling that she should be with her own people who were suffering in the travails that came with the war. She got as far as England and there helped with the Free French movement. Her efforts to return to France were not successful. She was hospitalised with tuberculosis, a condition that might have improved if she had fully cooperated with the treatment. However, in August 1943, she died of cardiac failure in Ashford in Kent. She was only 34 years of age.

Simone was perhaps like many a 'saint,' – not easy to appreciate. She could be given to a certain dogmatism and in much of her writing there is a disdain for the body and bodily existence. It was known that while she was in England she refused to eat more food than she knew her compatriots in France were allocated. Her philosophical rejection of the Old Testament led some to see her as a Gnostic and maybe not as close to orthodox Christianity as others thought. Nevertheless, there is a beautiful integrity to Simone's life that makes her one of the great spiritual figures of the 20th century. Her first English biographer, Richard Rees, sums up by saying 'as for her death, whatever explanation one may give it will amount in the end to saying that she died of love.'